ARTH...

was born in the Harlem section of Manhattan in 1915 and went to public schools there. He attended the University of Michigan where he wrote two plays a year and earned several money prizes and awards. On his return to New York after graduation he continued to write plays and worked in radio. A novelist and short-storywriter of distinction, he turned his major talents to writing for the theater, and in 1949 DEATH OF A SALESMAN received the Pulitzer Prize. His next major play was THE CRUCIBLE (1953) followed by A VIEW FROM THE BRIDGE (1955), which received the Gold Medal Award for Drama from the National Institute of Arts and Letters.

Mr. Miller's more recent works include AFTER THE FALL and INCIDENT AT VICHY, both of which were performed by the Lincoln Center Repertory in New York.

Plays by Arthur Miller

ALL MY SONS

DEATH OF A SALESMAN

❦ THE CRUCIBLE

❦ A VIEW FROM THE BRIDGE

ARTHUR MILLER'S COLLECTED PLAYS

❦ AFTER THE FALL

❦ INCIDENT AT VICHY

❦ Published by Bantam Books, Inc.

A VIEW
FROM THE BRIDGE
A play in two acts with an introduction
BY ARTHUR MILLER

*This low-priced Bantam Book
has been completely reset in a type face
designed for easy reading, and was printed
from new plates. It contains the complete
text of the original hard-cover edition.*
NOT ONE WORD HAS BEEN OMITTED.

A VIEW FROM THE BRIDGE
*A Bantam Book / published by arrangement with
The Viking Press, Inc.*

PRINTING HISTORY
Viking edition published November 1955
Book Find Club (alternate) edition published December 1955
Fireside Theatre Club edition published June 1956
Included in Viking Press Collected Plays edition May 1957
2nd printing . . . February 1958
3rd printing . . . February 1959
4th printing . . . . . May 1960
Viking Press (Compass) edition published June 1960
2nd printing . . . May 1961
Bantam edition published December 1961
Bantam Library of World Drama edition published January 1967

INTRODUCTION

A play is rarely given a second chance. Unlike a
novel, which may be received initially with less than
enthusiasm, and then as time goes by hailed by a
large public, a play usually makes its mark right off or
it vanishes into oblivion. Two of mine, *The Crucible*
and *A View from the Bridge,* failed to find large audi-
ences with their original Broadway productions. Both
were regarded as rather cold plays at first. However,
after a couple of years *The Crucible* was produced
again off Broadway and ran two years, without a line
being changed from the original. With McCarthy dead
it was once again possible to feel warmly toward the
play, whereas during his time of power it was sus-
pected of being a special plea, a concoction and un-
aesthetic. On its second time around its humanity
emerged and it could be enjoyed as drama.

At this writing I have not permitted a second
New York production of *A View from the Bridge*
principally because I have not had the desire to see
it through the mill a second time. However, a year
or so after its first production it was done with great
success in London and then in Paris, where it ran two
years. It is done everywhere in this country without
any apparent difficulty in reaching the emotions of
the audience. This play, however, unlike *The Crucible,*
I have revised, and it was the revision which London
and Paris saw. The nature of the revisions bears directly upon the questions of form and style which
interest students and theater workers.

The original play produced on Broadway (Viking, 1955) was in one act. It was a hard, telegraphic, unadorned drama. Nothing was permitted which did not advance the progress of Eddie's catastrophe in a most direct way. In a Note to the published play, I wrote: "What struck me first about this tale when I heard it one night in my neighborhood was how directly, with what breathtaking simplicity, it did evolve. It seemed to me, finally, that its very bareness, its absolutely unswerving path, its exposed skeleton, so to speak, was its wisdom and even its charm and must not be tampered with. . . . These *qualities* of the events themselves, their texture, seemed to me more psychologically telling than a conventional investigation in width which would necessarily relax that clear, clean line of his catastrophe."

The explanation for this point of view lies in great part in the atmosphere of the time in which the play was written. It seemed to me then that the theater was retreating into an area of psycho-sexual romanticism, and this at the very moment when great events both at home and abroad cried out for recognition and analytic inspection. In a word, I was tired of mere sympathy in the theater. The spectacle of still another misunderstood victim left me impatient. The tender emotions, I felt, were being overworked. I wanted to write in a way that would call up the faculties of knowing as well as feeling. To bathe the audience in tears, to grip people by the age-old methods of suspense, to theatricalize life, in a word, seemed faintly absurd to me if not disgusting.

In *The Crucible* I had taken a step, I felt, toward a more self-aware drama. The Puritan not only felt, but constantly referred his feelings to concepts, to codes and ideas of social and ethical importance. Feeling, it seemed to me, had to be made of importance; the dramatic victory had to be more than a triumph over the audience's indifference. It must call up a concept, a new awareness.

I had known the story of *A View from the Bridge* for a long time. A water-front worker who had known Eddie's prototype told it to me. I had never thought to make a play of it because it was too complete, there was nothing I could add. And then a time came when its very completeness became appealing. It suddenly seemed to me that I ought to deliver it onto the stage as fact; that interpretation was inherent in the very existence of the tale in the first place. I saw that the reason I had not written it was that as a whole its meaning escaped me. I could not fit it into myself. It existed apart from me and seemed not to express anything within me. Yet it refused to disappear.

I wrote it in a mood of experiment—to see what it might mean. I kept to the *tale*, trying not to change its original shape. I wanted the audience to feel toward it as I had on hearing it for the first time—not so much with heart-wringing sympathy as with wonder. For when it was told to me I knew its ending a few minutes after the teller had begun to speak. I wanted to create suspense but not by withholding information. It must be suspenseful because one knew too well how it would come out, so that the basic feeling would be the desire to stop this man and tell him what he was really doing to his life. Thus, by knowing more than the hero, the audience would rather automatically see his life through conceptualized feelings.

As a consequence of this viewpoint, the characters were not permitted to talk about this and that before getting down to their functions in the tale; when a character entered he proceeded directly to serve the catastrophe. Thus, normal naturalistic acting techniques had to be modified. Excessive and arbitrary gestures were eliminated; the set itself was shorn of every adornment. An atmosphere was attempted in which nothing existed but the purpose of the tale.

The trouble was that neither the director, the actors, nor I had had any experience with this kind of staging. It was difficult to know how far to go. We were all aware that a strange style was called for which we were unsure how to provide.

About a year later in London new conditions created new solutions. Seemingly inconsequential details suggested these solutions at times. For one, the British actors could not reproduce the Brooklyn argot and had to create one that was never heard on heaven or earth. Already naturalism was evaporated by this much: the characters were slightly strange beings in a world of their own. Also, the pay scales of the London theater made it possible to do what I could not do in New York—hire a crowd.

These seemingly mundane facts had important consequences. The mind of Eddie Carbone is not comprehensible apart from its relation to his neighborhood, his fellow workers, his social situation. His self-esteem depends upon their estimate of him, and his value is created largely by his fidelity to the code of his culture. In New York we could have only four strategically placed actors to represent the community. In London there were at least twenty men and women surrounding the main action. Peter Brook, the British director, could then proceed to design a set which soared to the roof with fire escapes, passageways, suggested apartments, so that one sensed that Eddie was living out his horror in the midst of a certain normality, and that, invisibly and without having to speak of it, he was getting ready to invoke upon himself the wrath of his tribe. A certain size accrued to him as a result. The importance of his interior psychological dilemma was magnified to the size it would have in life. What had seemed like a mere aberration had now risen to a fatal violation of an ancient law. By the presence of his neighbors alone the play and Eddie were made more humanly understandable and moving. There was also the fact that the British cast, accustomed to playing Shakespeare, could incorporate into a seemingly realistic style the conception of the play—they moved easily into the larger-than-life attitude which the play demanded, and without the self-conscious awkwardness, the uncertain stylishness which hounds many actors without classic training.

As a consequence of not having to work at making the play seem as factual, as bare as I had conceived it, I felt now that it could afford to include elements of simple human motivation which I had rigorously excluded before—specifically, the viewpoint of Eddie's wife, and *her* dilemma in relation to him. This, in fact, accounts for almost all the added material which made it necessary to break the play in the middle for an intermission. In other words, once Eddie had been placed squarely in his social context, among his people, the mythlike feeling of the story emerged of itself, and he could be made more human and less a figure, a force. It thus seemed quite in keeping that certain details of realism should be allowed; a Christmas tree and decorations in the living room, for one, and a realistic make-up, which had been avoided in New York, where the actor was always much cleaner than a longshoreman ever is. In a word, the nature of the British actor and of the production there made it possible to concentrate more upon realistic characterization while the universality of Eddie's type was strengthened at the same time.

But it was not only external additions, such as a new kind of actor, sets, and so forth, which led to the expansion of the play. As I have said, the original was written in the hope that I would understand what it meant to me. It was only during the latter part of its run in New York that, while watching a performance one afternoon, I saw my own involvement in this story. Quite suddenly the play seemed to be "mine" and not merely a story I had heard. The revisions subsequently made were in part the result of that new awareness.

In general, then, I think it can be said that by the addition of significant psychological and behavioral detail the play became not only more human, warmer and less remote, but also a clearer statement. Eddie is still not a man to weep over; the play does not attempt to swamp an audience in tears. But it is more possible now to relate his actions to our own and thus to understand ourselves a little better not only as isolated psychological entities, but as we connect to our fellows and our long past together.

ARTHUR MILLER

March 1960

A VIEW FROM THE BRIDGE

CHARACTERS

Louis

Mike

Alfieri

Eddie

Catherine

Beatrice

Marco

Tony

Rodolpho

First Immigration Officer

Second Immigration Officer

Mr. Lipari

Mrs. Lipari

Two "Submarines"

Neighbors

*The street and house front of a tenement build-
ing. The front is skeletal entirely. The main acting
area is the living room—dining room of Eddie's apartment. It is a worker's flat, clean, sparse, homely. There
is a rocker down front; a round dining table at center,
with chairs; and a portable phonograph.*

*At back are a bedroom door and an opening to
the kitchen; none of these interiors are seen.*

*At the right, forestage, a desk. This is Mr.
Alfieri's law office.*

*There is also a telephone booth. This is not used
until the last scenes, so it may be covered or left in
view.*

*A stairway leads up to the apartment, and then
farther up to the next story, which is not seen.*

*Ramps, representing the street, run upstage and
off to right and left.*

*As the curtain rises, Louis and Mike, longshore-
men, are pitching coins against the building at left.*

A distant foghorn blows.

*Enter Alfieri, a lawyer in his fifties turning gray;
he is portly, good-humored, and thoughtful. The two
pitchers nod to him as he passes. He crosses the stage
to his desk, removes his hat, runs his fingers through
his hair, and grinning, speaks to the audience.*

ALFIERI
You wouldn't have known it, but something amus-
ing has just happened. You see how uneasily they
nod to me? That's because I am a lawyer. In this

3

neighborhood to meet a lawyer or a priest on the street is unlucky. We're only thought of in connection with disasters, and they'd rather not get too close.

I often think that behind that suspicious little nod of theirs lie three thousand years of distrust. A lawyer means the law, and in Sicily, from where their fathers came, the law has not been a friendly idea since the Greeks were beaten.

I am inclined to notice the ruins in things, perhaps because I was born in Italy. . . . I only came here when I was twenty-five. In those days, Al Capone, the greatest Carthaginian of all, was learning his trade on these pavements, and Frankie Yale himself was cut precisely in half by a machine gun on the corner of Union Street, two blocks away. Oh, there were many here who were justly shot by unjust men. Justice is very important here.

But this is Red Hook, not Sicily. This is the slum that faces the bay on the seaward side of Brooklyn Bridge. This is the gullet of New York swallowing the tonnage of the world. And now we are quite civilized, quite American. Now we settle for half, and I like it better. I no longer keep a pistol in my filing cabinet.

And my practice is entirely unromantic.

My wife has warned me, so have my friends; they tell me the people in this neighborhood lack elegance, glamour. After all, who have I dealt with in my life? Longshoremen and their wives, and fathers and grandfathers, compensation cases, evictions, family squabbles —the petty troubles of the poor—and yet . . . every few years there is still a case, and as the parties tell me what the trouble is, the flat air in my office suddenly washes in with the green scent of the sea, the dust in this air is blown away and the thought comes that in some Caesar's year, in Calabria perhaps or on the cliff at Syracuse, another lawyer, quite differently dressed, heard the same complaint and set there as powerless as I, and watched it run its bloody course.

Eddie has appeared and has been pitching coins

4

with the men and is highlighted among them. He is forty—a husky, slightly overweight longshoreman.

This one's name was Eddie Carbone, a longshoreman working the docks from Brooklyn Bridge to the breakwater where the open sea begins.

Alfieri walks into darkness.

EDDIE
(moving up steps into doorway)
Well, I'll see ya, fellas.

Catherine enters from kitchen, crosses down to window, looks out.

LOUIS
You workin' tomorrow?

EDDIE
Yeah, there's another day yet on that ship. See ya, Louis.

Eddie goes into the house, as light rises in the apartment.

Catherine is waving to Louis from the window and turns to him.

CATHERINE
Hi, Eddie!

Eddie is pleased and therefore shy about it; he hangs up his cap and jacket.

EDDIE
Where you goin' all dressed up?

CATHERINE
(running her hands over her skirt)
I just got it. You like it?

EDDIE
Yeah, it's nice. And what happened to your hair?

CATHERINE
You like it? I fixed it different. *Calling to kitchen:* He's here, B.!

EDDIE

Beautiful. Turn around, lemme see in the back. *She turns for him.* Oh, if your mother was alive to see you now! She wouldn't believe it.

CATHERINE

You like it, huh?

EDDIE

You look like one of them girls that went to college. Where you goin'?

CATHERINE
(taking his arm)

Wait'll B. comes in, I'll tell you something. Here, sit down. *She is walking him to the armchair. Calling offstage:* Hurry up, will you, B.?

EDDIE
(sitting)

What's goin' on?

CATHERINE

I'll get you a beer, all right?

EDDIE

Well, tell me what happened. Come over here, talk to me.

CATHERINE

I want to wait till B. comes in. *She sits on her heels beside him.* Guess how much we paid for the skirt.

EDDIE

I think it's too short, ain't it?

CATHERINE
(standing)

No! not when I stand up.

EDDIE

Yeah, but you gotta sit down sometimes.

CATHERINE

Eddie, it's the style now. *She walks to show him.* I mean, if you see me walkin' down the street—

EDDIE

Listen, you been givin' me the willies the way you walk down the street, I mean it.

CATHERINE

Why?

EDDIE

Catherine, I don't want to be a pest, but I'm tellin' you you're walkin' wavy.

CATHERINE

I'm walkin' wavy?

EDDIE

Now don't aggravate me, Katie, you are walkin' wavy! I don't like the looks they're givin' you in the candy store. And with them new high heels on the sidewalk—clack, clack, clack. The heads are turnin' like windmills.

CATHERINE

But those guys look at all the girls, you know that.

EDDIE

You ain't "all the girls."

CATHERINE

(almost in tears because he disapproves)
What do you want me to do? You want me to—

EDDIE

Now don't get mad, kid.

CATHERINE

Well, I don't know what you want from me.

EDDIE

Katie, I promised your mother on her deathbed. I'm responsible for you. You're a baby, you don't understand these things. I mean like when you stand here by the window, wavin' outside.

CATHERINE

I was wavin' to Louis!

EDDIE

Listen, I could tell you things about Louis which you wouldn't wave to him no more.

CATHERINE
(trying to joke him out of his warning)
Eddie, I wish there was one guy you couldn't tell me things about!

EDDIE

Catherine, do me a favor, will you? You're gettin' to be a big girl now, you gotta keep yourself more, you can't be so friendly, kid. *Calls:* Hey, B., what're you doin' in there? *To Catherine:* Get her in here, will you? I got news for her.

CATHERINE
(starting out)
What?

EDDIE

Her cousins landed.

CATHERINE
(clapping her hands together)
No! *She turns instantly and starts for the kitchen.* B.! Your cousins!
Beatrice enters, wiping her hands with a towel.

BEATRICE
(in the face of Catherine's shout)
What?

CATHERINE
Your cousins got in!

BEATRICE
(astounded, turns to Eddie)
What are you talkin' about? Where?

EDDIE

I was just knockin' off work before and Tony Bereli come over to me; he says the ship is in the North River.

8

BEATRICE

*(her hands are clasped at her breast; she seems half
in fear, half in unutterable joy)*
They're all right?

EDDIE

He didn't see them yet, they're still on board. But
as soon as they get off he'll meet them. He figures
about ten o'clock they'll be here.

BEATRICE
(sits, almost weak from tension)
And they'll let them off the ship all right? That's
fixed, heh?

EDDIE

Sure, they give them regular seamen papers and
they walk off with the crew. Don't worry about it, B.,
there's nothin' to it. Couple of hours they'll be here.

BEATRICE

What happened? They wasn't supposed to be till
next Thursday.

EDDIE

I don't know; they put them on any ship they can
get them out on. Maybe the other ship they was supposed to take there was some danger— What you
cryin' about?

BEATRICE
(astounded and afraid)
I'm— I just—I can't believe it! I didn't even buy a
new tablecloth; I was gonna wash the walls—

EDDIE

Listen, they'll think it's a millionaire's house com-
pared to the way they live. Don't worry about the
walls. They'll be thankful. *To Catherine:* Whyn't you
run down buy a tablecloth. Go ahead, here. *He is
reaching into his pocket.*

CATHERINE
There's no stores open now.

EDDIE
(to Beatrice)
You was gonna put a new cover on the chair.

BEATRICE
I know—well, I thought it was gonna be next week!
I was gonna clean the walls, I was gonna wax the
floors. *She stands disturbed.*

CATHERINE
(pointing upward)
Maybe Mrs. Dondero upstairs—

BEATRICE
(of the tablecloth)
No, hers is worse than this one. *Suddenly:* My God,
I don't even have nothin' to eat for them! *She starts
for the kitchen.*

EDDIE
(reaching out and grabbing her arm)
Hey, hey! Take it easy.

BEATRICE
No, I'm just nervous, that's all. *To Catherine:* I'll
make the fish.

EDDIE
You're savin' their lives, what're you worryin' about
the tablecloth? They probably didn't see a tablecloth
in their whole life where they come from.

BEATRICE
(looking into his eyes)
I'm just worried about you, that's all I'm worried.

EDDIE
Listen, as long as they know where they're gonna
sleep.

BEATRICE
I told them in the letters. They're sleepin' on the
floor.

EDDIE

Beatrice, all I'm worried about is you got such a heart that I'll end up on the floor with you, and they'll be in our bed.

BEATRICE

All right, stop it.

EDDIE

Because as soon as you see a tired relative, I end up on the floor.

BEATRICE

When did you end up on the floor?

EDDIE

When your father's house burned down I didn't end up on the floor?

BEATRICE

Well, their house burned down!

EDDIE

Yeah, but it didn't keep burnin' for two weeks!

BEATRICE

All right, look, I'll tell them to go someplace else. *She starts into the kitchen.*

EDDIE

Now just a minute. Beatrice! *She halts. He goes to her.* I just don't want you bein' pushed around, that's all. You got too big a heart. *He touches her hand.* What're you so touchy?

BEATRICE

I'm just afraid if it don't turn out good you'll be mad at me.

EDDIE

Listen, if everybody keeps his mouth shut, nothin' can happen. They'll pay for their board.

BEATRICE

Oh, I told them.

EDDIE

Then what the hell. *Pause. He moves.* It's an honor,
B. I mean it. I was just thinkin' before, comin' home,
suppose my father didn't come to this country, and I
was starvin' like them over there . . . and I had people
in America could keep me a couple of months? The
man would be honored to lend me a place to sleep.

BEATRICE

(there are tears in her eyes. She turns to Catherine)
You see what he is? *She turns and grabs Eddie's
face in her hands.* Mmm! You're an angel! God'll bless
you. *He is gratefully smiling.* You'll see, you'll get a
blessing for this!

EDDIE
(laughing)
I'll settle for my own bed.

BEATRICE

Go, Baby, set the table.

CATHERINE

We didn't tell him about me yet.

BEATRICE

Let him eat first, then we'll tell him. Bring everything in. *She hurries Catherine out.*

EDDIE
(sitting at the table)
What's all that about? Where's she goin'?

BEATRICE

Noplace. It's very good news, Eddie. I want you to
be happy.

EDDIE

What's goin' on?
Catherine enters with plates, forks.

BEATRICE

She's got a job.
*Pause. Eddie looks at Catherine, then back to
Beatrice.*

EDDIE

What job? She's gonna finish school.

CATHERINE

Eddie, you won't believe it—

EDDIE

No—no, you gonna finish school. What kinda job, what do you mean? All of a sudden you—

CATHERINE

Listen a minute, it's wonderful.

EDDIE

It's not wonderful. You'll never get nowheres unless you finish school. You can't take no job. Why didn't you ask me before you take a job?

BEATRICE

She's askin' you now, she didn't take nothin' yet.

CATHERINE

Listen a minute! I came to school this morning and the principal called me out of the class, see? To go to his office.

EDDIE

Yeah?

CATHERINE

So I went in and he says to me he's got my records, y'know? And there's a company wants a girl right away. It ain't exactly a secretary, it's a stenographer first, but pretty soon you get to be secretary. And he says to me that I'm the best student in the whole class—

BEATRICE

You hear that?

EDDIE

Well why not? Sure she's the best.

CATHERINE

I'm the best student, he says, and if I want, I should take the job and the end of the year he'll let me take the examination and he'll give me the certificate. So I'll save practically a year!

EDDIE
(strangely nervous)
Where's the job? What company?

CATHERINE
It's a big plumbing company over Nostrand Avenue.

EDDIE
Nostrand Avenue and where?

CATHERINE
It's someplace by the Navy Yard.

BEATRICE
Fifty dollars a week, Eddie.

EDDIE
(to Catherine, surprised)
Fifty?

CATHERINE
I swear.
Pause.

EDDIE
What about all the stuff you wouldn't learn this year, though?

CATHERINE
There's nothin' more to learn, Eddie, I just gotta practice from now on. I know all the symbols and I know the keyboard. I'll just get faster, that's all. And when I'm workin' I'll keep gettin' better and better, you see?

BEATRICE
Work is the best practice anyway.

EDDIE
That ain't what I wanted, though.

CATHERINE
Why! It's a great big company—

EDDIE

I don't like that neighborhood over there.

CATHERINE

It's a block and half from the subway, he says.

EDDIE

Near the Navy Yard plenty can happen in a block and a half. And a plumbin' company! That's one step over the water front. They're practically longshoremen.

BEATRICE

Yeah, but she'll be in the office, Eddie.

EDDIE

I know she'll be in the office, but that ain't what I had in mind.

BEATRICE

Listen, she's gotta go to work sometime.

EDDIE

Listen, B., she'll be with a lotta plumbers? And sailors up and down the street? So what did she go to school for?

CATHERINE

But it's fifty a week, Eddie.

EDDIE

Look, did I ask you for money? I supported you this long I support you a little more. Please, do me a favor, will ya? I want you to be with different kind of people. I want you to be in a nice office. Maybe a lawyer's office someplace in New York in one of them nice buildings. I mean if you're gonna get outa here then get out; don't go practically in the same kind of neighborhood.

Pause. Catherine lowers her eyes.

BEATRICE

Go, Baby, bring in the supper. *Catherine goes out.* Think about it a little bit, Eddie. Please. She's crazy to start work. It's not a little shop, it's a big company.

Some day she could be a secretary. They picked her out of the whole class. *He is silent, staring down at the tablecloth, fingering the pattern.* What are you worried about? She could take care of herself. She'll get out of the subway and be in the office in two minutes.

EDDIE
(somehow sickened)
I know that neighborhood, B., I don't like it.

BEATRICE
Listen, if nothin' happened to her in this neighborhood it ain't gonna happen noplace else. *She turns his face to her.* Look, you gotta get used to it, she's no baby no more. Tell her to take it. *He turns his head away.* You hear me? *She is angering.* I don't understand you; she's seventeen years old, you gonna keep her in the house all her life?

EDDIE
(insulted)
What kinda remark is that?

BEATRICE
(with sympathy but insistent force)
Well, I don't understand when it ends. First it was gonna be when she graduated high school, so she graduated high school. Then it was gonna be when she learned stenographer, so she learned stenographer. So what're we gonna wait for now? I mean it, Eddie, sometimes I don't understand you; they picked her out of the whole class, it's an honor for her.

Catherine enters with food, which she silently sets on the table. After a moment of watching her face, Eddie breaks into a smile, but it almost seems that tears will form in his eyes.

EDDIE
With your hair that way you look like a madonna, you know that? You're the madonna type. *She doesn't*

look at him, but continues ladling out food onto the plates. You wanna go to work, heh, Madonna?

CATHERINE
(softly)

Yeah.

EDDIE
(with a sense of her childhood, her babyhood, and the years)

All right, go to work. *She looks at him, then rushes and hugs him.* Hey, hey! Take it easy! *He holds her face away from him to look at her.* What're you cryin' about? *He is affected by her, but smiles his emotion away.*

CATHERINE
(sitting at her place)

I just—*Bursting out:* I'm gonna buy all new dishes with my first pay! *They laugh warmly.* I mean it. I'll fix up the whole house! I'll buy a rug!

EDDIE

And then you'll move away.

CATHERINE

No, Eddie!

EDDIE
(grinning)

Why not? That's life. And you come visit on Sundays, then once a month, then Christmas and New Year's, finally.

CATHERINE
(grasping his arm to reassure him and to erase the accusation)

No, please!

EDDIE
(smiling but hurt)

I only ask you one thing—don't trust nobody. You got a good aunt but she's got too big a heart, you learned bad from her. Believe me.

BEATRICE

Be the way you are, Katie, don't listen to him.

EDDIE

(to Beatrice—strangely and quickly resentful)
You lived in a house all your life, what do you know about it? You never worked in your life.

BEATRICE

She likes people. What's wrong with that?

EDDIE

Because most people ain't people. She's goin' to work; plumbers; they'll chew her to pieces if she don't watch out. *To Catherine:* Believe me, Katie, the less you trust, the less you be sorry.

Eddie crosses himself and the women do the same, and they eat.

CATHERINE

First thing I'll buy is a rug, heh, B.?

BEATRICE

I don't mind. *To Eddie:* I smelled coffee all day today. You unloadin' coffee today?

EDDIE

Yeah, a Brazil ship.

CATHERINE

I smelled it too. It smelled all over the neighborhood.

EDDIE

That's one time, boy, to be a longshoreman is a pleasure. I could work coffee ships twenty hours a day. You go down in the hold, y'know? It's like flowers, that smell. We'll bust a bag tomorrow, I'll bring you some.

BEATRICE

Just be sure there's no spiders in it, will ya? I mean it. *She directs this to Catherine, rolling her eyes upward.* I still remember that spider coming out of that bag he brung home. I nearly died.

EDDIE

You call that a spider? You oughta see what comes outa the bananas sometimes.

BEATRICE

Don't talk about it!

EDDIE

I seen spiders could stop a Buick.

BEATRICE

(clapping her hands over her ears)
All right, shut up!

EDDIE

(laughing and taking a watch out of his pocket)
Well, who started with spiders?

BEATRICE

All right, I'm sorry, I didn't mean it. Just don't bring none home again. What time is it?

EDDIE

Quarter nine. *Puts watch back in his pocket. They continue eating in silence.*

CATHERINE

He's bringin' them ten o'clock, Tony?

EDDIE

Around, yeah. *He eats.*

CATHERINE

Eddie, suppose somebody asks if they're livin' here. *He looks at her as though already she had divulged something publicly. Defensively:* I mean if they ask.

EDDIE

Now look, Baby, I can see we're gettin' mixed up again here.

CATHERINE

No, I just mean . . . people'll see them goin' in and out.

19

EDDIE

I don't care who sees them goin' in and out as long as you don't see them goin' in and out. And this goes for you too, B. You don't see nothin' and you don't know nothin'.

BEATRICE

What do you mean? I understand.

EDDIE

You don't understand; you still think you can talk about this to somebody just a little bit. Now lemme say it once and for all, because you're makin' me nervous again, both of you. I don't care if somebody comes in the house and sees them sleepin' on the floor, it never comes out of your mouth who they are or what they're doin' here.

BEATRICE

Yeah, but my mother'll know—

EDDIE

Sure she'll know, but just don't you be the one who told her, that's all. This is the United States government you're playin' with now, this is the Immigration Bureau. If you said it you knew it, if you didn't say it you didn't know it.

CATHERINE

Yeah, but Eddie, suppose somebody—

EDDIE

I don't care what question it is. You—don't—know—nothin'. They got stool pigeons all over this neighborhood they're payin them every week for information, and you don't know who they are. It could be your best friend. You hear? *To Beatrice:* Like Vinny Bolzano, remember Vinny?

BEATRICE

Oh, yeah. God forbid.

EDDIE

Tell her about Vinny. *To Catherine:* You think I'm blowin' steam here? *To Beatrice:* Go ahead, tell her. *To Catherine:* You was a baby then. There was a family next door to her mother, he was about sixteen—

BEATRICE

No, he was no more than fourteen, cause I was to his confirmation in Saint Agnes. But the family had an uncle that they were hidin' in the house, and he snitched to the Immigration.

CATHERINE

The kid snitched?

EDDIE

On his own uncle!

CATHERINE

What, was he crazy?

EDDIE

He was crazy after, I tell you that, boy.

BEATRICE

Oh, it was terrible. He had five brothers and the old father. And they grabbed him in the kitchen and pulled him down the stairs—three flights his head was bouncin' like a coconut. And they spit on him in the street, his own father and his brothers. The whole neighborhood was cryin'.

CATHERINE

Ts! So what happened to him?

BEATRICE

I think he went away. *To Eddie:* I never seen him again, did you?

EDDIE

(rises during this, taking out his watch)

Him? You'll never see him no more, a guy do a thing like that? How's he gonna show his face? *To Catherine, as he gets up uneasily:* Just remember, kid, you can quicker get back a million dollars that

21

was stole than a word that you gave away. *He is standing now, stretching his back.*

CATHERINE

Okay, I won't say a word to nobody, I swear.

EDDIE

Gonna rain tomorrow. We'll be slidin' all over the decks. Maybe you oughta put something on for them, they be here soon.

BEATRICE

I only got fish, I hate to spoil it if they ate already. I'll wait, it only takes a few minutes; I could broil it.

CATHERINE

What happens, Eddie, when that ship pulls out and they ain't on it, though? Don't the captain say nothin'?

EDDIE

(slicing an apple with his pocket knife)
Captain's pieced off, what do you mean?

CATHERINE

Even the captain?

EDDIE

What's the matter, the captain don't have to live? Captain gets a piece, maybe one of the mates, piece for the guy in Italy who fixed the papers for them, Tony here'll get a little bite. . . .

BEATRICE

I just hope they get work here, that's all I hope.

EDDIE

Oh, the syndicate'll fix jobs for them; till they pay 'em off they'll get them work every day. It's after the pay-off, then they'll have to scramble like the rest of us.

BEATRICE

Well, it be better than they got there.

EDDIE

Oh sure, well, listen. So you gonna start Monday, heh, Madonna?

CATHERINE
(embarrassed)
I'm supposed to, yeah.

Eddie is standing facing the two seated women. First Beatrice smiles, then Catherine, for a powerful emotion is on him, a childish one and a knowing fear, and the tears show in his eyes—and they are shy before the avowal.

EDDIE
(sadly smiling, yet somehow proud of her)
Well . . . I hope you have good luck. I wish you the best. You know that, kid.

CATHERINE
(rising, trying to laugh)
You sound like I'm goin' a million miles!

EDDIE
I know. I guess I just never figured on one thing.

CATHERINE
(smiling)
What?

EDDIE
That you would ever grow up. *He utters a soundless laugh at himself, feeling his breast pocket of his shirt.* I left a cigar in my other coat, I think. *He starts for the bedroom.*

CATHERINE
Stay there! I'll get it for you.

She hurries out. There is a slight pause, and Eddie turns to Beatrice, who has been avoiding his gaze.

EDDIE
What are you mad at me lately?

BEATRICE

Who's mad? *She gets up, clearing the dishes.* I'm not mad. *She picks up the dishes and turns to him.* You're the one is mad. *She turns and goes into the kitchen as Catherine enters from the bedroom with a cigar and a pack of matches.*

CATHERINE

Here! I'll light it for you! *She strikes a match and holds it to his cigar. He puffs. Quietly:* Don't worry about me, Eddie, heh?

EDDIE

Don't burn yourself. *Just in time she blows out the match.* You better go in help her with the dishes.

CATHERINE

(turns quickly to the table, and, seeing the table cleared, she says, almost guiltily)
Oh! *She hurries into the kitchen, and as she exits there:* I'll do the dishes, B.!
Alone, Eddie stands looking toward the kitchen for a moment. Then he takes out his watch, glances at it, replaces it in his pocket, sits in the arrmchair, and stares at the smoke flowing out of his mouth.
The lights do down, then come up on Alfieri, who has moved onto the forestage.

ALFIERI

He was as good a man as he had to be in a life that was hard and even. He worked on the piers when there was work, he brought home his pay, and he lived. And toward ten o'clock of that night, after they had eaten, the cousins came.
The lights fade on Alfieri and rise on the street.
Enter Tony, escorting Marco and Rodolpho, each with a valise. Tony halts, indicates the house. They stand for a moment looking at it.

MARCO

(he is a square-built peasant of thirty-two, suspicious, tender, and quiet voiced)

Thank you.

TONY

You're on your own now. Just be careful that's all. Ground floor.

MARCO

Thank you.

TONY

(indicating the house)

I'll see you on the pier tomorrow. You'll go to work.
    Marco nods. Tony continues on walking down the street.

RODOLPHO

This will be the first house I ever walked into in America! Imagine! She said they were poor!

MARCO

Ssh! Come. *They go to door.*
    Marco knocks. The lights rise in the room. Eddie goes and opens the door. Enter Marco and Rodolpho, removing their caps. Beatrice and Catherine enter from the kitchen. The lights fade in the street.

EDDIE

You Marco?

MARCO

Marco.

EDDIE

Come on in! *He shakes Marco's hand.*

BEATRICE

Here, take the bags!

MARCO

(nods, looks to the women and fixes on Beatrice. Crosses to Beatrice)

Are you my cousin?
    She nods. He kisses her hand.

BEATRICE
(above the table, touching her chest with her hand)
Beatrice. This is my husband, Eddie. *All nod.*
Catherine, my sister Nancy's daughter. *The brothers nod.*

MARCO
(indicating Rodolpho)
My brother. Rodolpho. *Rodolpho nods. Marco comes with a certain formal stiffness to Eddie.* I want to tell you now Eddie—when you say go, we will go.

EDDIE
Oh, no . . . *Takes Marco's bag.*

MARCO
I see it's a small house, but soon, maybe, we can have our own house.

EDDIE
You're welcome, Marco, we got plenty of room here. Katie, give them supper, heh? *Exits into bedroom with their bags.*

CATHERINE
Come here, sit down. I'll get you some soup.

MARCO
(as they go to the table)
We ate on the ship. Thank you. *To Eddie, calling off to bedroom:* Thank you.

BEATRICE
Get some coffee. We'll all have coffee. Come sit down.
Rodolpho and Marco sit, at the table.

CATHERINE
(wondrously)
How come he's so dark and you're so light, Rodolpho?

RODOLPHO
(ready to laugh)

I don't know. A thousand years ago, they say, the Danes invaded Sicily.

Beatrice kisses Rodolpho. They laugh as Eddie enters.

CATHERINE
(to Beatrice)

He's practically blond!

EDDIE

How's the coffee doin'?

CATHERINE
(brought up)

I'm gettin' it. *She hurries out to kitchen.*

EDDIE
(sits on his rocker)

Yiz have a nice trip?

MARCO

The ocean is always rough. But we are good sailors.

EDDIE

No trouble gettin' here?

MARCO

No. The man brought us. Very nice man.

RODOLPHO
(to Eddie)

He says we start to work tomorrow. Is he honest?

EDDIE
(laughing)

No. But as long as you owe them money, they'll get you plenty of work. *To Marco:* Yiz ever work on the piers in Italy?

MARCO

Piers? Ts!—no.

RODOLPHO
(smiling at the smallness of his town)
In our town there are no piers, only the beach, and
little fishing boats.

BEATRICE
So what kinda work did yiz do?

MARCO
(shrugging shyly, even embarrassed)
Whatever there is, anything.

RODOLPHO
Sometimes they build a house, or if they fix the
bridge—Marco is a mason and I bring him the
cement. *He laughs.* In harvest time we work in the
fields . . . if there is work. Anything.

EDDIE
Still bad there, heh?

MARCO
Bad, yes.

RODOLPHO
(laughing)
It's terrible! We stand around all day in the piazza
listening to the fountain like birds. Everybody waits
only for the train.

BEATRICE
What's on the train?

RODOLPHO
Nothing. But if there are many passengers and
you're lucky you make a few lire to push the taxi up
the hill.
Enter Catherine; she listens.

BEATRICE
You gotta push a taxi?

RODOLPHO
(laughing)
Oh, sure! It's a feature in our town. The horses in
our town are skinnier than goats. So if there are too

28

many passengers we help push the carriages up to the hotel. *He laughs.* In our town the horses are only for show.

CATHERINE

Why don't they have automobile taxis?

RODOLPHO

There is one. We push that too. *They laugh.* Everything in our town, you gotta push!

BEATRICE
(to Eddie)

How do you like that!

EDDIE
(to Marco)

So what're you wanna do, you gonna stay here in this country or you wanna go back?

MARCO
(surprised)

Go back?

EDDIE

Well, you're married, ain't you?

MARCO

Yes. I have three children.

BEATRICE

Three! I thought only one.

MARCO

Oh, no. I have three now. Four years, five years, six years.

BEATRICE

Ah . . . I bet they're cryin' for you already, heh?

MARCO

What can I do? The older one is sick in his chest. My wife—she feeds them from her own mouth. I tell you the truth, if I stay there they will never grow up. They eat the sunshine.

BEATRICE

My God. So how long you want to stay?

MARCO

With your permission, we will stay maybe a—

EDDIE

She don't mean in this house, she means in the country.

MARCO

Oh. Maybe four, five, six years, I think.

RODOLPHO
(smiling)

He trusts his wife.

BEATRICE

Yeah, but maybe you'll get enough, you'll be able to go back quicker.

MARCO

I hope. I don't know. *To Eddie:* I understand it's not so good here either.

EDDIE

Oh, you guys'll be all right—till you pay them off, anyway. After that, you'll have to scramble, that's all. But you'll make better here than you could there.

RODOLPHO

How much? We hear all kinds of figures. How much can a man make? We work hard, we'll work all day, all night—
Marco raises a hand to hush him.

EDDIE
(he is coming more and more to address Marco only)

On the average a whole year? Maybe—well, it's hard to say, see. Sometimes we lay off, there's no ships three four weeks.

MARCO

Three, four weeks!—Ts!

EDDIE

But I think you could probably—thirty, forty a week, over the whole twelve months of the year.

MARCO
(rises, crosses to Eddie)
Dollars.

EDDIE

Sure dollars.

Marco puts an arm around Rodolpho and they laugh.

MARCO

If we can stay here a few months, Beatrice—

BEATRICE

Listen, you're welcome, Marco—

MARCO

Because I could send them a little more if I stay here.

BEATRICE

As long as you want, we got plenty a room.

MARCO
(his eyes are showing tears)
My wife—*To Eddie:* My wife—I want to send right away maybe twenty dollars—

EDDIE

You could send them something next week already.

MARCO
(he is near tears)
Eduardo . . . *He goes to Eddie, offering his hand.*

EDDIE

Don't thank me. Listen, what the hell, it's no skin off me. *To Catherine:* What happened to the coffee?

CATHERINE

I got it on. *To Rodolpho:* You married too? No.

RODOLPHO
(rises)

Oh, no . . .

BEATRICE
(to Catherine)

I told you he—

CATHERINE

I know, I just thought maybe he got married recently.

RODOLPHO

I have no money to get married. I have a nice face, but no money. *He laughs.*

CATHERINE
(to Beatrice)

He's a real blond!

BEATRICE
(to Rodolpho)

You want to stay here too, heh? For good?

RODOLPHO

Me? Yes, forever! Me, I want to be an American. And then I want to go back to Italy when I am rich, and I will buy a motorcycle. *He smiles. Marco shakes him affectionately.*

CATHERINE

A motorcycle!

RODOLPHO

With a motorcycle in Italy you will never starve any more.

BEATRICE

I'll get you coffee. *She exits to the kitchen.*

EDDIE

What you do with a motorcycle?

MARCO

He dreams, he dreams.

RODOLPHO
(to Marco)

Why? *To Eddie:* Messages! The rich people in the hotel always need someone who will carry a message. But quickly, and with a great noise. With a blue motorcycle I would station myself in the courtyard of the hotel, and in a little while I would have messages.

MARCO

When you have no wife you have dreams.

EDDIE

Why can't you just walk, or take a trolley or sump'm?
Enter Beatrice with coffee.

RODOLPHO

Oh, no, the machine, the machine is necessary. A man comes into a great hotel and says, I am a messenger. Who is this man? He disappears walking, there is no noise, nothing. Maybe he will never come back, maybe he will never deliver the message. But a man who rides up on a great machine, this man is responsible, this man exists. He will be given messages. *He helps Beatrice set out the coffee things.* I am also a singer, though.

EDDIE

You mean a regular—?

RODOLPHO

Oh, yes. One night last year Andreola got sick. Baritone. And I took his place in the garden of the hotel. Three arias I sang without a mistake! Thousand-lire notes they threw from the tables, money was falling like a storm in the treasury. It was magnificent. We lived six months on that night, eh, Marco?
Marco nods doubtfully.

MARCO

Two months.
Eddie laughs.

BEATRICE
Can't you get a job in that place?

RODOLPHO
Andreola got better. He's a baritone, very strong.
Beatrice laughs.

MARCO
(regretfully, to Beatrice)
He sang too loud.

RODOLPHO
Why too loud?

MARCO
Too loud. The guests in that hotel are all Englishmen. They don't like too loud.

RODOLPHO
(to Catherine)
Nobody ever said it was too loud!

MARCO
I say. It was too loud. *To Beatrice:* I knew it as soon as he started to sing. Too loud.

RODOLPHO
Then why did they throw so much money?

MARCO
They paid for your courage. The English like courage. But once is enough.

RODOLPHO
(to all but Marco)
I never heard anybody say it was too loud.

CATHERINE
Did you ever hear of jazz?

RODOLPHO
Oh, sure! I *sing* jazz.

CATHERINE
(rises)
You could sing jazz?

34

RODOLPHO

Oh, I sing Napolidan, jazz, bel canto—I sing "Paper Doll," you like "Paper Doll"?

CATHERINE

Oh, sure, I'm crazy for "Paper Doll." Go ahead, sing it.

RODOLPHO

(takes his stance after getting a nod of permission from Marco, and with a high tenor voice begins singing)

"I'll tell you boys it's tough to be alone,
And it's tough to love a doll that's not your own.
I'm through with all of them,
I'll never fall again,
Hey, boy, what you gonna do?
I'm gonna buy a paper doll that I can call my own,
A doll that other fellows cannot steal.
    Eddie rises and moves upstage.
And then those flirty, flirty guys
With their flirty, flirty eyes
Will have to flirt with dollies that are real—

EDDIE

Hey, kid—hey, wait a minute—

CATHERINE
(enthralled)
Leave him finish, it's beautiful! *To Beatrice:* He's terrific! It's terrific, Rodolpho.

EDDIE

Look, kid; you don't want to be picked up, do ya?

MARCO

No—no! *He rises.*

EDDIE
(indicating the rest of the building)
Because we never had no singers here . . . and all of a sudden there's a singer in the house, y'know what I mean?

MARCO

Yes, yes. You'll be quiet, Rodolpho.

EDDIE

(he is flushed)
They got guys all over the place, Marco. I mean.

MARCO

Yes. He'll be quiet. *To Rodolpho:* You'll be quiet.
Rodolpho nods.
Eddie has risen, with iron control, even a smile.
He moves to Catherine.

EDDIE

What's the high heels for, Garbo?

CATHERINE

I figured for tonight—

EDDIE

Do me a favor, will you? Go ahead.
*Embarrassed now, angered, Catherine goes out
into the bedroom. Beatrice watches her go and gets
up; in passing, she gives Eddie a cold look, restrained
only by the strangers, and goes to the table to pour
coffee.*

EDDIE

*(striving to laugh, and to Marco, but directed as much
to Beatrice)*
All actresses they want to be around here.

RUDOLPHO

(happy about it)
In Italy too! All the girls.
*Catherine emerges from the bedroom in low-heel
shoes, comes to the table. Rodolpho is lifting a cup.*

EDDIE

*(he is sizing up Rodolpho, and there is a concealed
suspicion)*
Yeah, heh?

RODOLPHO

Yes! *Laughs, indicating Catherine:* Especially when they are so beautiful!

CATHERINE

You like sugar?

RODOLPHO

Sugar? Yes! I like sugar very much!

Eddie is downstage, watching as she pours a spoonful of sugar into his cup, his face puffed with trouble, and the room dies.

Lights rise on Alfieri.

ALFIERI

Who can ever know what will be discovered? Eddie Carbone had never expected to have a destiny. A man works, raises his family, goes bowling, eats, gets old, and then he dies. Now, as the weeks passed, there was a future, there was a trouble that would not go away.

The lights fade on Alfieri, then rise on Eddie standing at the doorway of the house. Beatrice enters on the street. She sees Eddie, smiles at him. He looks away.

She starts to enter the house when Eddie speaks.

EDDIE

It's after eight.

BEATRICE

Well, it's a long show at the Paramount.

EDDIE

They must've seen every picture in Brooklyn by now. He's supposed to stay in the house when he ain't working. He ain't supposed to go advertising himself.

BEATRICE

Well that's his trouble, what do you care? If they pick him up they pick him up, that's all. Come in the house.

EDDIE

What happened to the stenography? I don't see her practice no more.

BEATRICE

She'll get back to it. She's excited, Eddie.

EDDIE

She tell you anything?

BEATRICE

(comes to him, now the subject is opened)
What's the matter with you? He's a nice kid, what do you want from him?

EDDIE

That's a nice kid? He gives me the heeby-jeebies.

BEATRICE

(smiling)
Ah, go on, you're just jealous.

EDDIE

Of *him?* Boy, you don't think much of me.

BEATRICE

I don't understand you. What's so terrible about him?

EDDIE

You mean it's all right with you? That's gonna be her husband?

BEATRICE

Why? He's a nice fella, hard workin', he's a good-lookin' fella.

EDDIE

He sings on the ships, didja know that?

BEATRICE

What do you mean, he sings?

EDDIE

Just what I said, he sings. Right on the deck, all of a sudden, a whole song comes out of his mouth—

with motions. You know what they're calling him now? Paper Doll they're callin' him, Canary. He's like a weird. He comes out on the pier, one-two-three, it's a regular show.

BEATRICE

Well, he's a kid; he don't know how to behave himself yet.

EDDIE

And with that wacky hair; he's like a chorus girl or sump'n.

BEATRICE

So he's blond, so—

EDDIE

I just hope that's his regular hair, that's all I hope.

BEATRICE

You crazy or sump'n? *She tries to turn him to her.*

EDDIE

(he keeps his head turned away)
What's so crazy? I don't like his whole way.

BEATRICE

Listen, you never seen a blond guy in your life? What about Whitey Balso?

EDDIE

(turning to her victoriously)
Sure, but Whitey don't sing; he don't do like that on the ships.

BEATRICE

Well, maybe that's the way they do in Italy.

EDDIE

Then why don't his brother sing? Marco goes around like a man; nobody kids Marco. *He moves from her, halts. She realizes there is a campaign solidified in him.* I tell you the truth I'm surprised I have to tell you all this. I mean I'm surprised, B.

BEATRICE
(she goes to him with purpose now)
Listen, you ain't gonna start nothin' here.

EDDIE
I ain't startin' nothin', but I ain't gonna stand around lookin' at that. For that character I didn't bring her up. I swear, B., I'm surprised at you; I sit there waitin' for you to wake up but everything is great with you.

BEATRICE
No, everything ain't great with me.

EDDIE
No?

BEATRICE
No. But I got other worries.

EDDIE
Yeah. *He is already weakening.*

BEATRICE
Yeah, you want me to tell you?

EDDIE
(in retreat)
Why? What worries you got?

BEATRICE
When am I gonna be a wife again, Eddie?

EDDIE
I ain't been feelin' good. They bother me since they came.

BEATRICE
It's almost three months you don't feel good; they're only here a couple of weeks. It's three months, Eddie.

EDDIE
I don't know, B. I don't want to talk about it.

BEATRICE
What's the matter, Eddie, you don't like me, heh?

EDDIE

What do you mean, I don't like you? I said I don't feel good, that's all.

BEATRICE

Well, tell me, am I doing something wrong? Talk to me.

EDDIE

(Pause. He can't speak, then)
I can't. I can't talk about it.

BEATRICE

Well tell me what—

EDDIE

I got nothin' to say about it!
She stands for a moment; he is looking off; she turns to go into the house.

EDDIE

I'll be all right, B; just lay off me, will ya? I'm worried about her.

BEATRICE

The girl is gonna be eighteen years old, it's time already.

EDDIE

B., he's taking her for a ride!

BEATRICE

All right, that's her ride. What're you gonna stand over her till she's forty? Eddie, I want you to cut it out now, you hear me? I don't like it! Now come in the house.

EDDIE

I want to take a walk, I'll be in right away.

BEATRICE

They ain't goin' to come any quicker if you stand in the street. It ain't nice, Eddie.

EDDIE

I'll be in right away. Go ahead. *He walks off.*
She goes into the house. Eddie glances up the

street, sees Louis and Mike coming, and sits on an iron railing. Louis and Mike enter.

LOUIS

Wanna go bowlin' tonight?

EDDIE

I'm too tired. Goin' to sleep.

LOUIS

How's your two submarines?

EDDIE

They're okay.

LOUIS

I see they're gettin' work allatime.

EDDIE

Oh, yeah, they're doin' all right.

MIKE

That's what we oughta do. We oughta leave the country and come in under the water. Then we get work.

EDDIE

You ain't kiddin'.

LOUIS

Well, what the hell. Y'know?

EDDIE

Sure.

LOUIS

(sits on railing beside Eddie)

Believe me, Eddie, you got a lotta credit comin' to you.

EDDIE

Aah, they don't bother me, don't cost me nutt'n.

MIKE

That older one, boy, he's a regular bull. I seen him the other day liftin' coffee bags over the Matson Line. They leave him alone he woulda load the whole ship by himself.

EDDIE

Yeah, he's a strong guy, that guy. Their father was a regular giant, supposed to be.

LOUIS

Yeah, you could see. He's a regular slave.

MIKE
(grinning)

That blond one, though—*Eddie looks at him.* He's got a sense of humor. *Louis snickers.*

EDDIE
(searchingly)

Yeah. He's funny—

MIKE
(starting to laugh)

Well he ain't exactly funny, but he's always like makin' remarks like, y'know? He comes around, everybody's laughin'. *Louis laughs.*

EDDIE
(uncomfortably, grinning)

Yeah, well . . . he's got a sense of humor.

MIKE
(laughing)

Yeah, I mean, he's always makin' like remarks, like, y'know?

EDDIE

Yeah, I know. But he's a kid yet, y'know? He—he's just a kid, that's all.

MIKE
(getting hysterical with Louis)

I know. You take one look at him—everybody's happy. *Louis laughs.* I worked one day with him last week over the Moore-MacCormack Line, I'm tell' you they was all hysterical. *Louis and he explode in laughter.*

EDDIE

Why? What'd he do?

MIKE

I don't know . . . he was just humorous. You never can remember what he says, y'know? But it's the way he says it. I mean he gives you a look sometimes and you start laughin'!

EDDIE

Yeah. *Troubled:* He's got a sense of humor.

MIKE
(gasping)

Yeah.

LOUIS
(rising)

Well, we see ya, Eddie.

EDDIE

Take it easy.

LOUIS

Yeah. See ya.

MIKE

If you wanna come bowlin' later we're goin' Flatbush Avenue.

Laughing, they move to exit, meeting Rodolpho and Catherine entering on the street. Their laughter rises as they see Rodolpho, who does not understand but joins in. Eddie moves to enter the house as Louis and Mike exit. Catherine stops him at the door.

CATHERINE

Hey, Eddie—what a picture we saw! Did we laugh!

EDDIE
(he can't help smiling at sight of her)
Where'd you go?

CATHERINE

Paramount. It was with those two guys, y'know? That—

EDDIE

Brooklyn Paramount?

44

CATHERINE
(with an edge of anger, embarrassed before Rodolpho)
Sure, the Brooklyn Paramount. I told you we wasn't goin' to New York.

EDDIE
(retreating before the threat of her anger)
All right, I only asked you. *To Rodolpho:* I just don't want her hangin' around Times Square, see? It's full of tramps over there.

RODOLPHO
I would like to go to Broadway once, Eddie. I would like to walk with her once where the theaters are and the opera. Since I was a boy I see pictures of those lights.

EDDIE
(his little patience waning)
I want to talk to her a minute, Rodolpho. Go inside, will you?

RODOLPHO
Eddie, we only walk together in the streets. She teaches me.

CATHERINE
You know what he can't get over? That there's no fountains in Brooklyn!

EDDIE
(smiling unwillingly)
Fountains? *Rodolpho smiles at his own naïveté.*

CATHERINE
In Italy he says, every town's got fountains, and they meet there. And you know what? They got oranges on the trees where he comes from, and lemons. Imagine —on the trees? I mean it's interesting. But he's crazy for New York.

RODOLPHO
(attempting familiarity)
Eddie, why can't we go once to Broadway—?

EDDIE

Look, I gotta tell her something—

RODOLPHO

Maybe you can come too. I want to see all those lights. *He sees no response in Eddie's face. He glances at Catherine.* I'll walk by the river before I go to sleep. *He walks off down the street.*

CATHERINE

Why don't you talk to him, Eddie? He blesses you, and you don't talk to him hardly.

EDDIE

(enveloping her with his eyes)

I bless you and you don't talk to me. *He tries to smile.*

CATHERINE

I don't talk to you? *She hits his arm.* What do you mean?

EDDIE

I don't see you no more. I come home you're runnin' around someplace—

CATHERINE

Well, he wants to see everything, that's all, so we go. . . . You mad at me?

EDDIE

No. *He moves from her, smiling sadly.* It's just I used to come home, you was always there. Now, I turn around, you're a big girl. I don't know how to talk to you.

CATHERINE

Why?

EDDIE

I don't know, you're runnin', you're runnin', Katie. I don't think you listening any more to me.

CATHERINE
(going to him)
Ah, Eddie, sure I am. What's the matter? You don't like him?
Slight pause.

EDDIE
(turns to her)
You like him, Katie?

CATHERINE
(with a blush but holding her ground)
Yeah. I like him.

EDDIE
(his smile goes)
You like him.

CATHERINE
(looking down)
Yeah. *Now she looks at him for the consequences, smiling but tense. He looks at her like a lost boy.* What're you got against him? I don't understand. He only blesses you.

EDDIE
(turns away)
He don't bless me, Katie.

CATHERINE
He does! You're like a father to him!

EDDIE
(turns to her)
Katie.

CATHERINE
What, Eddie?

EDDIE
You gonna marry him?

CATHERINE
I don't know. We just been . . . goin' around, that's all. *Turns to him:* What're you got against him, Eddie? Please, tell me. What?

EDDIE

He don't respect you.

CATHERINE

Why?

EDDIE

Katie . . . if you wasn't an orphan, wouldn't he ask your father's permission before he run around with you like this?

CATHERINE

Oh, well, he didn't think you'd mind.

EDDIE

He knows I mind, but it don't bother him if I mind, don't you see that?

CATHERINE

No, Eddie, he's got all kinds of respect for me. And you too! We walk across the street he takes my arm—he almost bows to me! You got him all wrong, Eddie; I mean it, you—

EDDIE

Katie, he's only bowin' to his passport.

CATHERINE

His passport!

EDDIE

That's right. He marries you he's got the right to be an American citizen. That's what's goin' on here. *She is puzzled and surprised.* You understand what I'm tellin' you? The guy is lookin' for his break, that's all he's lookin' for.

CATHERINE
(pained)

Oh, no, Eddie, I don't think so.

EDDIE

You don't think so! Katie, you're gonna make me cry here. Is that a workin' man? What does he do with his first money? A snappy new jacket he buys, records, a pointy pair new shoes and his brother's kids are starvin' over there with tuberculosis? That's a hit-and-run guy, baby; he's got bright lights in his head, Broadway. Them guys don't think of nobody but theirself! You marry him and the next time you see him it'll be for divorce!

CATHERINE
(steps toward him)
Eddie, he never said a word about his papers or—

EDDIE
You mean he's supposed to tell you that?

CATHERINE
I don't think he's even thinking about it.

EDDIE
What's better for him to think about! He could be picked up any day here and he's back pushin' taxis up the hill!

CATHERINE
No, I don't believe it.

EDDIE
Katie, don't break my heart, listen to me.

CATHERINE
I don't want to hear it.

EDDIE
Katie, listen . . .

CATHERINE
He loves me!

EDDIE
(with deep alarm)
Don't say that, for God's sake! This is the oldest racket in the country—

CATHERINE
(desperately, as though he had made his imprint)
I don't believe it! *She rushes to the house.*

EDDIE
(following her)
They been pullin' this since the Immigration Law was put in! They grab a green kid that don't know nothin' and they—

CATHERINE
(sobbing)
I don't believe it and I wish to hell you'd stop it!

EDDIE
Katie!

They enter the apartment. The lights in the living room have risen and Beatrice is there. She looks past the sobbing Catherine at Eddie, who in the presence of his wife, makes an awkward gesture of eroded command, indicating Catherine.

EDDIE
Why don't you straighten her out?

BEATRICE
(inwardly angered at his flowing emotion which in itself alarms her)
When are you going to leave her alone?

EDDIE
B., the guy is no good!

BEATRICE
(suddenly, with open fright and fury)
You going to leave her alone? Or you gonna drive me crazy? He turns, striving to retain his dignity, but nevertheless in guilt walks out of the house, into the street and away. Catherine starts into a bedroom. Listen, Catherine. *Catherine halts, turns to her sheepishly.* What are you going to do with yourself?

CATHERINE
I don't know.

BEATRICE
Don't tell me you don't know; you're not a baby any more, what are you going to do with yourself?

CATHERINE

He won't listen to me.

BEATRICE

I don't understand this. He's not your father, Catherine. I don't understand what's going on here.

CATHERINE

(as one who herself is trying to rationalize a buried impulse)

What am I going to do, just kick him in the face with it?

BEATRICE

Look, honey, you wanna get married, or don't you wanna get married? What are you worried about, Katie?

CATHERINE

(quietly, trembling)

I don't know B. It just seems wrong if he's against it so much.

BEATRICE

(never losing her aroused alarm)

Sit down, honey, I want to tell you something. Here, sit down. Was there ever any fella he liked for you? There wasn't, was there?

CATHERINE

But he says Rodolpho's just after his papers.

BEATRICE

Look, he'll say anything. What does he care what he says? If it was a prince came here for you it would be no different. You know that, don't you?

CATHERINE

Yeah, I guess.

BEATRICE

So what does that mean?

CATHERINE

(slowly turns her head to Beatrice)

What?

BEATRICE

It means you gotta be your own self more. You still think you're a little girl, honey. But nobody else can make up your mind for you any more, you understand? You gotta give him to understand that he can't give you orders no more.

CATHERINE

Yeah, but how am I going to do that? He thinks I'm a baby.

BEATRICE

Because *you* think you're a baby. I told you fifty times already, you can't act the way you act. You still walk around in front of him in your slip—

CATHERINE

Well I forgot.

BEATRICE

Well you can't do it. Or like you sit on the edge of the bathtub talkin' to him when he's shavin' in his underwear.

CATHERINE

When'd I do that?

BEATRICE

I seen you in there this morning.

CATHERINE

Oh . . . well, I wanted to tell him something and I—

BEATRICE

I know, honey. But if you act like a baby and he be treatin' you like a baby. Like when he comes home sometimes you throw yourself at him like when you was twelve years old.

CATHERINE

Well I like to see him and I'm happy so I—

BEATRICE

Look, I'm not tellin' you what to do honey, but—

CATHERINE

No, you could tell me, B.! Gee, I'm all mixed up. See, I—He looks so sad now and it hurts me.

BEATRICE

Well look Katie, if it's goin' to hurt you so much you're gonna end up an old maid here.

CATHERINE

No!

BEATRICE

I'm telling you, I'm not makin' a joke. I tried to tell you a couple of times in the last year or so. That's why I was so happy you were going to go out and get work, you wouldn't be here so much, you'd be a little more independent. I mean it. It's wonderful for a whole family to love each other, but you're a grown woman and you're in the same house with a grown man. So you'll act different now, heh?

CATHERINE

Yeah, I will. I'll remember.

BEATRICE

Because it ain't only up to him, Katie, you understand? I told him the same thing already.

CATHERINE
(quickly)

What?

BEATRICE

That he should let you go. But, you see, if only I tell him, he thinks I'm just bawlin' him out, or maybe I'm jealous or somethin', you know?

CATHERINE
(astonished)

He said you was jealous?

BEATRICE

No, I'm just sayin' maybe that's what he thinks. *She reaches over to Catherine's hand; with a strained smile:* You think I'm jealous of you, honey?

CATHERINE
No! It's the first I thought of it.

BEATRICE
(with a quiet sad laugh)
Well you should have thought of it before . . . but I'm not. We'll be all right. Just give him to understand; you don't have to fight, you're just— You're a woman, that's all, and you got a nice boy, and now the time came when you said good-by. All right?

CATHERINE
(strangely moved at the prospect)
All right. . . . If I can.

BEATRICE
Honey . . . you gotta.
Catherine, sensing now an imperious demand, turns with some fear, with a discovery, to Beatrice. She is at the edge of tears, as though a familiar world had shattered.

CATHERINE
Okay.
Lights out on them and up on Alfieri, seated behind his desk.

ALFIERI
It was at this time that he first came to me. I had represented his father in an accident case some years before, and I was acquainted with the family in a casual way. I remember him now as he walked through my doorway—
Enter Eddie down right ramp.
His eyes were like tunnels; my first thought was that he had committed a crime.
Eddie sits beside the desk, cap in hand, looking out.
but soon I saw it was only a passion that had moved into his body, like a stranger. *Alfieri pauses, looks down at his desk, then to Eddie as though he were continuing a conversation with him.* I don't quite

understand what I can do for you. Is there a question of law somewhere?

EDDIE
That's what I want to ask you.

ALFIERI
Because there's nothing illegal about a girl falling in love with an immigrant.

EDDIE
Yeah, but what about it if the only reason for it is to get his papers?

ALFIERI
First of all you don't know that.

EDDIE
I see it in his eyes; he's laughin' at her and he's laughin' at me.

ALFIERI
Eddie, I'm a lawyer. I can only deal in what's provable. You understand that, don't you? Can you prove that?

EDDIE
I know what's in his mind, Mr. Alfieri!

ALFIERI
Eddie, even if you could prove that—

EDDIE
Listen . . . will you listen to me a minute? My father always said you was a smart man. I want you to listen to me.

ALFIERI
I'm only a lawyer, Eddie.

EDDIE
Will you listen a minute? I'm talkin' about the law. Lemme just bring out what I mean. A man, which he comes into the country illegal, don't it stand to reason he's gonna take every penny and put it in the sock? Because they don't know from one day to another, right?

ALFIERI

All right.

EDDIE

He's spendin'. Records he buys now. Shoes. Jackets.
Y'understand me? This guy ain't worried. This guy is
here. So it must be that he's got it all laid out in his
mind already—he's stayin'. Right?

ALFIERI

Well? What about it?

EDDIE

All right. *He glances at Alfieri, then down to the
floor.* I'm talking to you confidential, ain't I?

ALFIERI

Certainly.

EDDIE

I mean it don't go no place but here. Because I
don't like to say this about anybody. Even my wife I
didn't exactly say this.

ALFIERI

What is it?

EDDIE

*(takes a breath and glances briefly over each
shoulder)*
The guy ain't right, Mr. Alfieri.

ALFIERI

What do you mean?

EDDIE

I mean he ain't right.

ALFIERI

I don't get you.

EDDIE

(shifts to another position in the chair)
Dja ever get a look at him?

ALFIERI

Not that I know of, no.

EDDIE

He's a blond guy. Like . . . platinum. You know what I mean?

ALFIERI

No.

EDDIE

I mean if you close the paper fast—you could blow him over.

ALFIERI

Well that doesn't mean—

EDDIE

Wait a minute, I'm tellin' you sump'm. He sings, see. Which is— I mean it's all right, but sometimes he hits a note, see. I turn around. I mean—high. You know what I mean?

ALFIERI

Well, that's a tenor.

EDDIE

I know a tenor, Mr. Alfieri. This ain't no tenor. I mean if you came in the house and you didn't know who was singin', you wouldn't be lookin' for him you be lookin' for her.

ALFIERI

Yes, but that's not—

EDDIE

I'm tellin' you sump'm, wait a minute. Please, Mr. Alfieri. I'm tryin' to bring out my thoughts here. Couple of nights ago my niece brings out a dress which it's too small for her, because she shot up like a light this last year. He takes the dress, lays it on the table, he cuts it up; one-two-three, he makes a new dress. I mean he looked so sweet there, like an angel— you could kiss him he was so sweet.

ALFIERI

Now look, Eddie—

EDDIE

Mr. Alfieri, they're laughin' at him on the piers. I'm ashamed. Paper Doll they call him. Blondie now. His brother thinks it's because he's got a sense of humor, see—which he's got—but that ain't what they're laughin'. Which they're not goin' to come out with it because they know he's my relative, which they have to see me if they make a crack, y'know? But I know what they're laughin' at, and when I think of that guy layin' his hands on her I could— I mean it's eatin' me out, Mr. Alfieri, because I struggled for that girl. And now he comes in my house and—

ALFIERI

Eddie, look—I have my own children. I understand you. But the law is very specific. The law does not . . .

EDDIE

(with a fuller flow of indignation)

You mean to tell me that there's no law that a guy which he ain't right can go to work and marry a girl and—?

ALFIERI

You have no recourse in the law, Eddie.

EDDIE

Yeah, but if he ain't right, Mr. Alfieri, you mean to tell me—

ALFIERI

There is nothing you can do, Eddie, believe me.

EDDIE

Nothin'.

ALFIERI

Nothing at all. There's only one legal question here.

EDDIE

What?

ALFIERI

The manner in which they entered the country. But I don't think you want to do anything about that, do you?

EDDIE

You mean—?

ALFIERI

Well, they entered illegally.

EDDIE

Oh, Jesus, no, I wouldn't do nothin' about that, I mean—

ALFIERI

All right, then, let me talk now, eh?

EDDIE

Mr. Alfieri, I can't believe what you tell me. I mean there must be some kinda law which—

ALFIERI

Eddie, I want you to listen to me. *Pause.* You know, sometimes God mixes up the people. We all love somebody, the wife, the kids—every man's got somebody that he loves, heh? But sometimes . . . there's too much. You know? There's too much, and it goes where it mustn't. A man works hard, he brings up a child, sometimes it's a niece, sometimes even a daughter, and he never realizes it, but through the years—there is too much love for the daughter, there is too much love for the niece. Do you understand what I'm saying to you?

EDDIE

(sardonically)

What do you mean, I shouldn't look out for her good?

ALFIERI

Yes, but these things have to end, Eddie, that's all. The child has to grow up and go away, and the man has to learn to forget. Because after all, Eddie —what other way can it end? *Pause.* Let her go. That's my advice. You did your job, now it's her life; wish her luck, and let her go. *Pause.* Will you do that? Because there's no law, Eddie; make up your mind to it; the law is not interested in this.

EDDIE

You mean to tell me, even if he's a punk? If he's—

ALFIERI

There's nothing you can do.
Eddie stands.

EDDIE

Well, all right, thanks. Thanks very much.

ALFIERI

What are you going to do?

EDDIE

(with a helpless but ironic gesture)
What can I do? I'm a patsy, what can a patsy do? I worked like a dog twenty years so a punk could have her, so that's what I done. I mean, in the worst times, in the worst, when there wasn't a ship comin' in the harbor, I didn't stand around lookin' for relief—I hustled. When there was empty piers in Brooklyn I went to Hoboken, Staten Island, the West Side, Jersey, all over—because I made a promise. I took out of my own mouth to give to her. I took out of my wife's mouth. I walked hungry plenty days in this city! *It begins to break through.* And now I gotta sit in my house and look at a son-of-a-bitch punk like that— which he came out of nowhere! I give him my house to sleep! I take the blankets off my bed for him, and he takes and puts his dirty filthy hands on her like a goddam thief!

ALFIERI

(rising)
But, Eddie, she's a woman now.

EDDIE

He's stealing from me!

ALFIERI

She wants to get married, Eddie. She can't marry you, can she?

EDDIE
(furiously)
What're you talkin' about, marry me! I don't know what the hell you're talkin' about!
Pause.

ALFIERI
I gave you my advice, Eddie. That's it.
Eddie gathers himself. A pause.

EDDIE
Well, thanks. Thanks very much. It just—it's breakin' my heart, y'know. I—

ALFIERI
I understand. Put it out of your mind. Can you do that?

EDDIE
I'm— *He feels the threat of sobs, and with a helpless wave.* I'll see you around. *He goes out up the right ramp.*

ALFIERI
(sits on desk)
There are times when you want to spread an alarm, but nothing has happened. I knew, I knew then and there—I could have finished the whole story that afternoon. It wasn't as though there was a mystery to unravel. I could see every step coming, step after step, like a dark figure walking down a hall toward a certain door. I knew where he was heading for, I knew where he was going to end. And I sat here many afternoons asking myself why, being an intelligent man, I was so powerless to stop it. I even went to a certain old lady in the neighborhood, a very wise old woman, and I told her, and she only nodded, and said, "Pray for him . . ." And so I—waited here.

As lights go out on Alfieri, they rise in the apartment where all are finishing dinner. Beatrice and Catherine are clearing the table.

CATHERINE
You know where they went?

BEATRICE

Where?

CATHERINE

They went to Africa once. On a fishing boat. *Eddie glances at her.* It's true, Eddie.
Beatrice exits into the kitchen with dishes.

EDDIE

I didn't say nothin'. *He goes to his rocker, picks up a newspaper.*

CATHERINE

And I was never even in Staten Island.

EDDIE
(sitting with the paper)

You didn't miss nothin'. *Pause. Catherine takes dishes out.* How long that take you, Marco—to get to Africa?

MARCO
(rising)

Oh . . . two days. We go all over.

RODOLPHO
(rising)

Once we went to Yugoslavia.

EDDIE
(to Marco)

They pay all right on them boats?
Beatrice enters. She and Rodolpho stack the remaining dishes.

MARCO

If they catch fish they pay all right. *Sits on a stool.*

RODOLPHO

They're family boats, though. And nobody in our family owned one. So we only worked when one of the families was sick.

BEATRICE

Y'know, Marco, what I don't understand—there's an ocean full of fish and yiz are all starvin'.

EDDIE

They gotta have boats, nets, you need money.
Catherine enters.

BEATRICE

Yeah, but couldn't they like fish from the beach?
You see them down Coney Island—

MARCO

Sardines.

EDDIE

Sure. *Laughing.* How you gonna catch sardines on a
hook?

BEATRICE

Oh, I didn't know they're sardines. *To Catherine:*
They're sardines!

CATHERINE

Yeah, they follow them all over the ocean, Africa,
Yugoslavia . . . *She sits and begins to look through a
movie magazine. Rodolpho joins her.*

BEATRICE
(to Eddie)

It's funny, y'know. You never think of it, that sardines are swimming in the ocean! *She exits to kitchen
with dishes.*

CATHERINE

I know. It's like oranges and lemons on a tree. *To
Eddie:* I mean you ever think of oranges and lemons
on a tree?

EDDIE

Yeah, I know. It's funny. *To Marco:* I heard that
they paint the oranges to make them look orange.
Beatrice enters.

MARCO
(he has been reading a letter)

Paint?

EDDIE

Yeah, I heard that they grow like green.

MARCO

No, in Italy the oranges are orange.

RODOLPHO

Lemons are green.

EDDIE
(resenting his instruction)

I know lemons are green, for Christ's sake, you see them in the store they're green sometimes. I said oranges they paint, I didn't say nothin' about lemons.

BEATRICE
(sitting; diverting their attention)

Your wife is gettin' the money all right, Marco?

MARCO

Oh, yes. She bought medicine for my boy.

BEATRICE

That's wonderful. You feel better, heh?

MARCO

Oh, yes! But I'm lonesome.

BEATRICE

I just hope you ain't gonna do like some of them around here. They're here twenty-five years, some men, and they didn't get enough together to go back twice.

MARCO

Oh, I know. We have many families in our town, the children never saw the father. But I will go home. Three, four years, I think.

BEATRICE

Maybe you should keep more here. Because maybe she thinks it comes so easy you'll never get ahead of yourself.

MARCO

Oh, no, she saves. I send everything. My wife is very lonesome. *He smiles shyly.*

BEATRICE

She must be nice. She pretty? I bet, heh?

MARCO
(blushing)
No, but she understand everything.

RODOLPHO

Oh, he's got a clever wife!

EDDIE

I betcha there's plenty surprises sometimes when those guys get back there, heh?

MARCO

Surprises?

EDDIE
(laughing)
I mean, you know—they count the kids and there's a couple extra than when they left?

MARCO

No—no . . . The women wait, Eddie. Most. Most. Very few surprises.

RODOLPHO

It's more strict in our town. *Eddie looks at him now.* It's not so free.

EDDIE
(rises, paces up and down)
It ain't so free here either, Rodolpho, like you think. I seen greenhorns sometimes get in trouble that way—they think just because a girl don't go around with a shawl over her head that she ain't strict, y'know? Girl don't have to wear black dress to be strict. Know what I mean?

RODOLPHO

Well, I always have respect—

EDDIE

I know, but in your town you wouldn't just drag off some girl without permission, I mean. *He turns.*

You know what I mean, Marco? It ain't that much different here.

MARCO
(*cautiously*)

Yes.

BEATRICE

Well, he didn't exactly drag her off though, Eddie.

EDDIE

I know, but I seen some of them get the wrong idea sometimes. *To Rodolpho:* I mean it might be a little more free here but it's just as strict.

RODOLPHO

I have respect for her, Eddie. I do anything wrong?

EDDIE

Look, kid, I ain't her father, I'm only her uncle—

BEATRICE

Well then, be an uncle then. *Eddie looks at her, aware of her criticizing force.* I mean.

MARCO

No, Beatrice, if he does wrong you must tell him. *To Eddie:* What does he do wrong?

EDDIE

Well, Marco, till he came here she was never out on the street twelve o'clock at night.

MARCO
(*to Rodolpho*)

You come home early now.

BEATRICE
(*to Catherine*)

Well, you said the movie ended late, didn't you?

CATHERINE

Yeah.

BEATRICE

Well, tell him, honey. *To Eddie:* The movie ended late.

EDDIE

Look, B., I'm just sayin'—he thinks she always stayed out like that.

MARCO

You come home early now, Rodolpho.

RODOLPHO
(embarrassed)

All right, sure. But I can't stay in the house all the time, Eddie.

EDDIE

Look, kid, I'm not only talkin' about her. The more you run around like that the more chance you're takin'. *To Beatrice:* I mean suppose he gets hit by a car or something. *To Marco:* Where's his papers, who is he? Know what I mean?

BEATRICE

Yeah, but who is he in the daytime, though? It's the same chance in the daytime.

EDDIE
(holding back a voice full of anger)

Yeah, but he don't have to go lookin' for it, Beatrice. If he's here to work, then he should work; if he's here for a good time then he could fool around! *To Marco:* But I understood, Marco, that you was both comin' to make a livin' for your family. You understand me, don't you, Marco? *He goes to his rocker.*

MARCO

I beg your pardon, Eddie.

EDDIE

I mean, that's what I understood in the first place, see.

MARCO

Yes. That's why we came.

EDDIE
(sits on his rocker)
Well, that's all I'm askin'.
*Eddie reads his paper. There is a pause, an awk-
wardness. Now Catherine gets up and puts a record
on the phonograph—"Paper Doll."*

CATHERINE
(flushed with revolt)
You wanna dance, Rodolpho?
Eddie freezes.

RODOLPHO
(in deference to Eddie)
No, I—I'm tired.

BEATRICE
Go ahead, dance, Rodolpho.

CATHERINE
Ah, come on. They got a beautiful quartet, these
guys. Come.
*She has taken his hand and he stiffly rises, feeling
Eddie's eyes on his back, and they dance.*

EDDIE
(to Catherine)
What's that, a new record?

CATHERINE
It's the same one. We bought it the other day.

BEATRICE
(to Eddie)
They only bought three records. *She watches them
dance; Eddie turns his head away. Marco just sits
there, waiting. Now Beatrice turns to Eddie.* Must be
nice to go all over in one of them fishin' boats. I would
like that myself. See all them other countries?

EDDIE
Yeah.

BEATRICE
(to Marco)
But the women don't go along, I bet.

MARCO
No, not on the boats. Hard work.

BEATRICE
What're you got, a regular kitchen and everything?

MARCO
Yes, we eat very good on the boats—especially when Rodolpho comes along; everybody gets fat.

BEATRICE
Oh, he cooks?

MARCO
Sure, very good cook. Rice, pasta, fish, everything.
Eddie lowers his paper.

EDDIE
He's a cook, too! *Looking at Rodolpho:* He sings, he cooks . . .
Rodolpho smiles thankfully.

BEATRICE
Well, it's good, he could always make a living.

EDDIE
It's wonderful. He sings, he cooks, he could make dresses.

CATHERINE
They get some high pay, them guys. The head chefs in all the big hotels are men. You read about them.

EDDIE
That's what I'm sayin'.
Catherine and Rodolpho continue dancing.

CATHERINE
Yeah, well, I mean.

EDDIE

(to Beatrice)

He's lucky, believe me. *Slight pause. He looks away, then back to Beatrice.* That's why the water front is no place for him. *They stop dancing. Rodolpho turns off phonograph.* I mean like me—I can't cook, I can't sing, I can't make dresses, so I'm on the water front. But if I could cook, if I could sing, if I could make dresses, I wouldn't be on the water front. *He has been unconsciously twisting the newspaper into a tight roll. They are all regarding him now; he senses he is exposing the issue and he is driven on.* I would be someplace else. I would be like in a dress store. *He has bent the rolled paper and it suddenly tears in two. He suddenly gets up and pulls his pants up over his belly and goes to Marco.* What do you say, Marco, we go to the bouts next Saturday night. You never seen a fight, did you?

MARCO

(uneasily)

Only in the moving pictures.

EDDIE

(going to Rodolpho)

I'll treat yiz. What do you say, Danish? You wanna come along? I'll buy the tickets.

RODOLPHO

Sure. I like to go.

CATHERINE

(goes to Eddie; nervously happy now)

I'll make some coffee, all right?

EDDIE

Go ahead, make some! Make it nice and strong. *Mystified, she smiles and exits to kitchen. He is weirdly elated, rubbing his fists into his palms. He strides to Marco.* You wait, Marco, you see some real fights here. You ever do any boxing?

MARCO

No, I never.

EDDIE

(to Rodolpho)
Betcha you have done some, heh?

RODOLPHO

No.

EDDIE

Well, come on, I'll teach you.

BEATRICE

What's he got to learn that for?

EDDIE

Ya can't tell, one a these days somebody's liable to step on his foot or sump'm. Come on, Rodolpho, I show you a couple a passes. *He stands below table.*

BEATRICE

Go ahead, Rodolpho. He's a good boxer, he could teach you.

RODOLPHO

(embarrassed)
Well, I don't know how to—*He moves down to Eddie.*

EDDIE

Just put your hands up. Like this, see? That's right. That's very good, keep your left up, because you lead with the left, see, like this. *He gently moves his left into Rodolpho's face.* See? Now what you gotta do is you gotta block me, so when I come in like that you—*Rodolpho parries his left.* Hey, that's very good! *Rodolpho laughs.* All right, now come into me. Come on.

RODOLPHO

I don't want to hit you, Eddie.

EDDIE

Don't pity me, come on. Throw it, I'll show you how to block it. *Rodolpho jabs at him, laughing. The others join.* 'At's it. Come on again. For the jaw right here. *Rodolpho jabs with more assurance.* Very good!

BEATRICE
(to Marco)

He's very good!
Eddie crosses directly upstage of Rodolpho.

EDDIE

Sure, he's great! Come on, kid, put sump'm behind it, you can't hurt me. *Rodolpho, more seriously, jabs at Eddie's jaw and grazes it.* Attaboy.
Catherine comes from the kitchen, watches.
Now I'm gonna hit you, so block me, see?

CATHERINE
(with beginning alarm)

What are they doin'?
They are lightly boxing now.

BEATRICE
(she senses only the comradeship in it now)

He's teachin' him; he's very good!

EDDIE

Sure, he's terrific! Look at him go! *Rodolpho lands a blow.* 'At's it! Now, watch out, here I come, Danish! *He feints with his left hand and lands with his right. It mildly staggers Rodolpho. Marco rises.*

CATHERINE
(rushing to Rodolpho)

Eddie!

EDDIE

Why? I didn't hurt him. Did I hurt you, kid? *He rubs the back of his hand across his mouth.*

RODOLPHO

No, no, he didn't hurt me. *To Eddie with a certain gleam and a smile:* I was only surprised.

BEATRICE

(pulling Eddie down into the rocker)
That's enough, Eddie; he did pretty good, though.

EDDIE

Yeah. *Rubbing his fists together:* He could be very good, Marco. I'll teach him again.
Marco nods at him dubiously.

RODOLPHO

Dance, Catherine. Come. *He takes her hand; they go to phonograph and start it. It plays "Paper Doll."*
Rodolpho takes her in his arms. They dance. Eddie in thought sits in his chair, and Marco takes a chair, places it in front of Eddie, and looks down at it. Beatrice and Eddie watch him.

MARCO

Can you lift this chair?

EDDIE

What do you mean?

MARCO

From here. *He gets on one knee with one hand behind his back, and grasps the bottom of one of the chair legs but does not raise it.*

EDDIE

Sure, why not? *He comes to the chair, kneels, grasps the leg, raises the chair one inch, but it leans over to the floor.* Gee, that's hard, I never knew that. *He tries again, and again fails.* It's on an angle, that's why, heh?

MARCO

Here. *He kneels, grasps, and with strain slowly raises the chair higher and higher, getting to his feet now. Rodolpho and Catherine have stopped dancing as Marco raises the chair over his head.*
Marco is face to face with Eddie, a strained ten-

sion gripping his eyes and jaw, his neck stiff, the chair raised like a weapon over Eddie's head—and he transforms what might appear like a glare of warning into a smile of triumph, and Eddie's grin vanishes as he absorbs his look.

CURTAIN

ACT TWO

Light rises on Alfieri at his desk.

ALFIERI

On the twenty-third of that December a case of Scotch whisky slipped from a net while being unloaded—as a case of Scotch whisky is inclined to do on the twenty-third of December on Pier Forty-one. There was no snow, but it was cold, his wife was out shopping. Marco was still at work. The boy had not been hired that day; Catherine told me later that this was the first time they had been alone together in the house.

Light is rising on Catherine in the apartment. Rodolpho is watching as she arranges a paper pattern on cloth spread on the table.

CATHERINE

You hungry?

RODOLPHO

Not for anything to eat. *Pause.* I have nearly three hundred dollars. Catherine?

CATHERINE

I heard you.

RODOLPHO

You don't like to talk about it any more?

CATHERINE

Sure, I don't mind talkin' about it.

RODOLPHO

What worries you, Catherine?

CATHERINE

I been wantin' to ask you about something. Could I?

RODOLPHO

All the answers are in my eyes, Catherine. But you don't look in my eyes lately. You're full of secrets. *She looks at him. She seems withdrawn.* What is the question?

CATHERINE

Suppose I wanted to live in Italy.

RODOLPHO
(smiling at the incongruity)
You going to marry somebody rich?

CATHERINE

No, I mean live there—you and me.

RODOLPHO
(his smile vanishing)
When?

CATHERINE

Well . . . when we get married.

RODOLPHO
(astonished)
You want to be an Italian?

CATHERINE

No, but I could live there without being Italian. Americans live there.

RODOLPHO

Forever?

CATHERINE

Yeah.

RODOLPHO
(crosses to rocker)
You're fooling.

CATHERINE

No, I mean it.

RODOLPHO

Where do you get such an idea?

CATHERINE

Well, you're always saying it's so beautiful there, with the mountains and the ocean and all the—

RODOLPHO

You're fooling me.

CATHERINE

I mean it.

RODOLPHO

(goes to her slowly)

Catherine, if I ever brought you home with no money, no business, nothing, they would call the priest and the doctor and they would say Rodolpho is crazy.

CATHERINE

I know, but I think we would be happier there.

RODOLPHO

Happier! What would you eat? You can't cook the view!

CATHERINE

Maybe you could be a singer, like in Rome or—

RODOLPHO

Rome! Rome is full of singers.

CATHERINE

Well, I could work then.

RODOLPHO

Where?

CATHERINE

God, there must be jobs somewhere!

RODOLPHO

There's nothing! Nothing, nothing, nothing. Now tell me what you're talking about. How can I bring you from a rich country to suffer in a poor country? What are you talking about? *He searches for words.*

I would be a criminal stealing your face. In two years you would have an old, hungry face. When my brother's babies cry they give them water, water that boiled a bone. Don't you believe that?

CATHERINE
(quietly)
I'm afraid of Eddie here.
Slight pause.

RODOLPHO
(steps closer to her)
We wouldn't live here. Once I am a citizen I could work anywhere and I would find better jobs and we would have a house, Catherine. If I were not afraid to be arrested I would start to be something wonderful here!

CATHERINE
(steeling herself)
Tell me something. I mean just tell me, Rodolpho— would you still want to do it if it turned out we had to go live in Italy? I mean just if it turned out that way.

RODOLPHO
This is your question or his question?

CATHERINE
I would like to know, Rodolpho. I mean it.

RODOLPHO
To go there with nothing.

CATHERINE
Yeah.

RODOLPHO
No. *She looks at him wide-eyed.* No.

CATHERINE
You wouldn't?

RODOLPHO
No; I will not marry you to live in Italy. I want you to be my wife, and I want to be a citizen. Tell him

that, or I will. Yes. *He moves about angrily.* And tell him also, and tell yourself, please, that I am not a beggar, and you are not a horse, a gift, a favor for a poor immigrant.

CATHERINE

Well, don't get mad!

RODOLPHO

I am furious! *Goes to her.* Do you think I am so desperate? My brother is desperate, not me. You think I would carry on my back the rest of my life a woman I didn't love just to be an American? It's so wonderful? You think we have no tall buildings in Italy? Electric lights? No wide streets? No flags? No automobiles? Only work we don't have. I want to be an American so I can work, that is the only wonder here—work! How can you insult me, Catherine?

CATHERINE

I didn't mean that—

RODOLPHO

My heart dies to look at you. Why are you so afraid of him?

CATHERINE
(near tears)

I don't know!

RODOLPHO

Do you trust me, Catherine? You?

CATHERINE

It's only that I— He was good to me, Rodolpho. You don't know him; he was always the sweetest guy to me. Good. He razzes me all the time but he don't mean it. I know. I would—just feel ashamed if I made him sad. 'Cause I always dreamt that when I got married he would be happy at the wedding, and laughin'— and now he's—mad all the time and nasty— *She is weeping.* Tell him you'd live in Italy—just tell him, and maybe he would start to trust you a little, see?

Because I want him to be happy; I mean—I like him,
Rodolpho—and I can't stand it!

RODOLPHO

Oh, Catherine—oh, little girl.

CATHERINE

I love you, Rodolpho, I love you.

RODOLPHO

Then why are you afraid? That he'll spank you?

CATHERINE

Don't, don't laugh at me! I've been here all my
life. . . . Every day I saw him when he left in the
morning and when he came home at night. You think
it's so easy to turn around and say to a man he's
nothin' to you no more?

RODOLPHO

I know, but—

CATHERINE

You don't know; nobody knows! I'm not a baby,
I know a lot more than people think I know. Beatrice
says to be a woman, but—

RODOLPHO

Yes.

CATHERINE

Then why don't she be a woman? If I was a wife
I would make a man happy instead of goin' at him all
the time. I can tell a block away when he's blue in his
mind and just wants to talk to somebody quiet and
nice. . . . I can tell when he's hungry or wants a beer
before he even says anything. I know when his feet
hurt him, I mean I *know* him and now I'm supposed to
turn around and make a stranger out of him? I don't
know why I have to do that, I mean.

RODOLPHO

Catherine. If I take in my hands a little bird. And
she grows and wishes to fly. But I will not let her out

of my hands because I love her so much, is that right
for me to do? I don't say you must hate him; but anyway you must go, mustn't you? Catherine?

CATHERINE
(softly)

Hold me.

RODOLPHO
(clasping her to him)

Oh, my little girl.

CATHERINE

Teach me. *She is weeping.* I don't know anything,
teach me, Rodolpho, hold me.

RODOLPHO

There's nobody here now. Come inside. Come. *He
is leading her toward the bedrooms.* And don't cry
any more.

*Light rises on the street. In a moment Eddie
appears. He is unsteady, drunk. He mounts the stairs.
He enters the apartment, looks around, takes out a
bottle from one pocket, puts it on the table. Then
another bottle from another pocket, and a third from
an inside pocket. He sees the pattern and cloth, goes
over to it and touches it, and turns toward upstage.*

EDDIE

Beatrice? *He goes to the open kitchen door and
looks in.* Beatrice? Beatrice?

*Catherine enters from bedroom; under his gaze
she adjusts her dress.*

CATHERINE

You got home early.

EDDIE

Knocked off for Christmas early. *Indicating the pattern:* Rodolpho makin' you a dress?

CATHERINE

No. I'm makin' a blouse.

Rodolpho appears in the bedroom doorway.

Eddie sees him and his arm jerks slightly in shock.
Rodolpho nods to him testingly.

RODOLPHO

Beatrice went to buy present for her mother.
Pause.

EDDIE

Pack it up. Go ahead. Get your stuff and get outa
here. *Catherine instantly turns and walks toward the*
bedroom, and Eddie grabs her arm. Where you goin'?

CATHERINE

(trembling with fright)
I think I have to get out of here, Eddie.

EDDIE

No, you ain't goin' nowheres, he's the one.

CATHERINE

I think I can't stay here no more. *She frees her*
arm, steps back toward the bedroom. I'm sorry, Eddie.
She sees the tears in his eyes. Well, don't cry. I'll be
around the neighborhood; I'll see you. I just can't
stay here no more. You know I can't. *Her sobs of pity*
and love for him break her composure. Don't you
know I can't? You know that, don't you? *She goes to*
him. Wish me luck. *She clasps her hands prayerfully.*
Oh, Eddie, don't be like that!

EDDIE

You ain't goin' nowheres.

CATHERINE

Eddie, I'm not gonna be a baby any more! You—
He reaches out suddenly, draws her to him, and
as she strives to free herself he kisses her on the
mouth.

RODOLPHO

Don't! *He pulls Eddie's arm.* Stop that! Have respect for her!

EDDIE
(spun around by Rodolpho)
You want something?

RODOLPHO
Yes! She'll be my wife. That is what I want. My wife!

EDDIE
But what're you gonna be?

RODOLPHO
I show you what I be!

CATHERINE
Wait outside; don't argue with him!

EDDIE
Come on, show me! What're you gonna be? Show me!

RODOLPHO
(with tears of rage)
Don't say that to me!
Rodolpho flies at him in attack. Eddie pins his arms, laughing, and suddenly kisses him.

CATHERINE
Eddie! Let go, ya hear me! I'll kill you! Leggo of him!
She tears at Eddie's face and Eddie releases Rodolpho. Eddie stands there with tears rolling down his face as he laughs mockingly at Rodolpho. She is staring at him in horror. Rodolpho is rigid. They are like animals that have torn at one another and broken up without a decision, each waiting for the other's mood.

EDDIE
(to Catherine)
You see? *To Rodolpho:* I give you till tomorrow, kid. Get outa here. Alone. You hear me? Alone.

CATHERINE

I'm going with him, Eddie. *She starts toward Rodolpho.*

EDDIE

(indicating Rodolpho with his head)
Not with that. *She halts, frightened. He sits, still panting for breath, and they watch him helplessly as he leans toward them over the table.* Don't make me do nuttin', Catherine. Watch your step, submarine. By rights they oughta throw you back in the water. But I got pity for you. *He moves unsteadily toward the door, always facing Rodolpho.* Just get outa here and don't lay another hand on her unless you wanna go out feet first. *He goes out of the apartment.*

The lights go down, as they rise on Alfieri.

ALFIERI

On December twenty-seventh I saw him next. I normally go home well before six, but that day I sat around looking out my window at the bay, and when I saw him walking through my doorway, I knew why I had waited. And if I seem to tell this like a dream, it was that way. Several moments arrived in the course of the two talks we had when it occurred to me how—almost transfixed I had come to feel. I had lost my strength somewhere. *Eddie enters, removing his cap, sits in the chair, looks thoughtfully out.* I looked in his eyes more than I listened—in fact, I can hardly remember the conversation. But I will never forget how dark the room became when he looked at me; his eyes were like tunnels. I kept wanting to call the police, but nothing had happened. Nothing at all had really happened. *He breaks off and looks down at the desk. Then he turns to Eddie.* So in other words, he won't leave?

EDDIE

My wife is talkin' about renting a room upstairs for them. An old lady on the top floor is got an empty room.

ALFIERI

What does Marco say?

EDDIE

He just sits there. Marco don't say much.

ALFIERI

I guess they didn't tell him, heh? What happened?

EDDIE

I don't know; Marco don't say much.

ALFIERI

What does your wife say?

EDDIE

(unwilling to pursue this)

Nobody's talkin' much in the house. So what about that?

ALFIERI

But you didn't prove anything about him. It sounds like he just wasn't strong enough to break your grip.

EDDIE

I'm tellin' you I know—he ain't right. Somebody that don't want it can break it. Even a mouse, if you catch a teeny mouse and you hold it in your hand, that mouse can give you the right kind of fight. He didn't give me the right kind of fight, I know it, Mr. Alfieri, the guy ain't right.

ALFIERI

What did you do that for, Eddie?

EDDIE

To show her what he is! So she would see, once and for all! Her mother'll turn over in the grave! *He gathers himself almost peremptorily.* So what do I gotta do now? Tell me what to do.

ALFIERI

She actually said she's marrying him?

EDDIE

She told me, yeah. So what do I do?
Slight pause.

ALFIERI

This is my last word, Eddie, take it or not, that's
your business. Morally and legally you have no rights,
you cannot stop it; she is a free agent.

EDDIE
(angering)
Didn't you hear what I told you?

ALFIERI
(with a tougher tone)
I heard what you told me, and I'm telling you what
the answer is. I'm not only telling you now, I'm warning you—the law is nature. The law is only a word
for what has a right to happen. When the law is
wrong it's because it's unnatural, but in this case it
is natural and a river will drown you if you buck it.
Let her go. And bless her. *A phone booth begins to
glow on the opposite side of the stage; a faint, lonely
blue. Eddie stands up, jaws clenched.* Somebody had
to come for her, Eddie, sooner or later. *Eddie starts
turning to go and Alfieri rises with new anxiety.* You
won't have a friend in the world, Eddie! Even those
who understand will turn against you, even the ones
who feel the same will despise you! *Eddie moves off.*
Put it out of your mind! Eddie! *He follows into the
darkness, calling desperately.*

*Eddie is gone. The phone is glowing in light
now. Light is out on Alfieri. Eddie has at the same
time appeared beside the phone.*

EDDIE

Give me the number of the Immigration Bureau.
Thanks. *He dials.* I want to report something. Illegal
immigrants. Two of them. That's right. Four-forty-one
Saxon Street, Brooklyn, yeah. Ground floor. Heh? *With*

greater difficulty: I'm just around the neighborhood, that's all. Heh?

Evidently he is being questioned further, and he slowly hangs up. He leaves the phone just as Louis and Mike come down the street.

LOUIS

Go bowlin', Eddie?

EDDIE

No, I'm due home.

LOUIS

Well, take it easy.

EDDIE

I'll see yiz.

They leave him, exiting right, and he watches them go. He glances about, then goes up into the house. The lights go on in the apartment. Beatrice is taking down Christmas decorations and packing them in a box.

EDDIE

Where is everybody? *Beatrice does not answer.* I says where is everybody?

BEATRICE
(looking up at him, wearied with it, and concealing a fear of him)

I decided to move them upstairs with Mrs. Dondero.

EDDIE

Oh, they're all moved up there already?

BEATRICE

Yeah.

EDDIE

Where's Catherine? She up there?

BEATRICE

Only to bring pillow cases.

EDDIE

She ain't movin' in with them.

87

BEATRICE

Look, I'm sick and tired of it. I'm sick and tired of it!

EDDIE

All right, all right, take it easy.

BEATRICE

I don't wanna hear no more about it, you understand? Nothin'!

EDDIE

What're you blowin' off about? Who brought them in here?

BEATRICE

All right, I'm sorry; I wish I'd a drop dead before I told them to come. In the ground I wish I was.

EDDIE

Don't drop dead, just keep in mind who brought them in here, that's all. *He moves about restlessly.* I mean I got a couple of rights here. *He moves, wanting to beat down her evident disapproval of him.* This is my house here not their house.

BEATRICE

What do you want from me? They're moved out; what do you want now?

EDDIE

I want my respect!

BEATRICE

So I moved them out, what more do you want? You got your house now, you got your respect.

EDDIE

(he moves about biting his lip)
I don't like the way you talk to me, Beatrice.

BEATRICE

I'm just tellin' you I done what you want!

EDDIE

I don't like it! The way you talk to me and the way you look at me. This is my house. And she is my niece and I'm responsible for her.

BEATRICE

So that's why you done that to him?

EDDIE

I done what to him?

BEATRICE

What you done to him in front of her; you know what I'm talkin' about. She goes around shakin' all the time, she can't go to sleep! That's what you call responsible for her?

EDDIE
(quietly)

The guy ain't right, Beatrice. *She is silent.* Did you hear what I said?

BEATRICE

Look, I'm finished with it. That's all. *She resumes her work.*

EDDIE
(helping her to pack the tinsel)

I'm gonna have it out with you one of these days, Beatrice.

BEATRICE

Nothin' to have out with me, it's all settled. Now we gonna be like it never happened, that's all.

EDDIE

I want my respect, Beatrice, and you know what I'm talkin' about.

BEATRICE

What?
Pause.

EDDIE
(finally his resolution hardens)

What I feel like doin' in the bed and what I don't feel like doin'. I don't want no—

BEATRICE

When'd I say anything about that?

EDDIE

You said, you said, I ain't deaf. I don't want no more conversations about that, Beatrice. I do what I feel like doin' or what I don't feel like doin'.

BEATRICE

Okay.
Pause.

EDDIE

You used to be different, Beatrice. You had a whole different way.

BEATRICE

I'm no different.

EDDIE

You didn't used to jump me all the time about everything. The last year or two I come in the house I don't know what's gonna hit me. It's a shootin' gallery in here and I'm the pigeon.

BEATRICE

Okay, okay.

EDDIE

Don't tell me okay, okay, I'm tellin' you the truth. A wife is supposed to believe the husband. If I tell you that guy ain't right don't tell me he is right.

BEATRICE

But how do you know?

EDDIE

Because I know. I don't go around makin' accusations. He give me the heeby-jeebies the first minute I seen him. And I don't like you sayin' I don't want her marryin' anybody. I broke my back payin' her stenography lessons so she could go out and meet a better class of people. Would I do that if I didn't want her to get married? Sometimes you talk like I was a crazy man or sump'm.

BEATRICE

But she likes him.

EDDIE

Beatrice, she's a baby, how is she gonna know what she likes?

BEATRICE

Well, you kept her a baby, you wouldn't let her go out. I told you a hundred times.
Pause.

EDDIE

All right. Let her go out, then.

BEATRICE

She don't wanna go out now. It's too late, Eddie.
Pause.

EDDIE

Suppose I told her to go out. Suppose I—

BEATRICE

They're going to get married next week, Eddie.

EDDIE
(his head jerks around to her)
She said that?

BEATRICE

Eddie, if you want my advice, go to her and tell her good luck. I think maybe now that you had it out you learned better.

EDDIE

What's the hurry next week?

BEATRICE

Well, she's been worried about him bein' picked up; this way he could start to be a citizen. She loves him, Eddie. *He gets up, moves about uneasily, restlessly.* Why don't you give her a good word? Because I still think she would like you to be a friend, y'know? *He is standing, looking at the floor.* I mean like if you told her you'd go to the wedding.

EDDIE

She asked you that?

BEATRICE

I know she would like it. I'd like to make a party for her. I mean there oughta be some kinda send-off. Heh? I mean she'll have trouble enough in her life, let's start it off happy. What do you say? Cause in her heart she still loves you, Eddie. I know it. *He presses his fingers against his eyes.* What're you, cryin'? *She goes to him, holds his face.* Go . . . whyn't you go tell her you're sorry? *Catherine is seen on the upper landing of the stairway, and they hear her descending.* There . . . she's comin' down. Come on, shake hands with her.

EDDIE

(moving with suppressed suddenness)
No, I can't, I can't talk to her.

BEATRICE

Eddie, give her a break; a wedding should be happy!

EDDIE

I'm goin', I'm goin' for a walk.
He goes upstage for his jacket. Catherine enters and starts for the bedroom door.

BEATRICE

Katie? . . . Eddie, don't go, wait a minute. *She embraces Eddie's arm with warmth.* Ask him, Katie. Come on, honey.

EDDIE

It's all right, I'm— *He starts to go and she holds him.*

BEATRICE

No, she wants to ask you. Come on, Katie, ask him. We'll have a party! What're we gonna do, hate each other? Come on!

CATHERINE

I'm gonna get married, Eddie. So if you wanna come, the wedding be on Saturday.

Pause.

EDDIE

Okay. I only wanted the best for you, Katie. I hope you know that.

CATHERINE

Okay. *She starts out again.*

EDDIE

Catherine? *She turns to him.* I was just tellin' Beatrice . . . if you wanna go out, like . . . I mean I realize maybe I kept you home too much. Because he's the first guy you ever knew, y'know? I mean now that you got a job, you might meet some fellas, and you get a different idea, y'know? I mean you could always come back to him, you're still only kids, the both of yiz. What's the hurry? Maybe you'll get around a little bit, you grow up a little more, maybe you'll see different in a couple of months. I mean you be surprised, it don't have to be him.

CATHERINE

No, we made it up already.

EDDIE

(with increasing anxiety)

Katie, wait a minute.

CATHERINE

No, I made up my mind.

EDDIE

But you never knew no other fella, Katie! How could you make up your mind?

CATHERINE

Cause I did. I don't want nobody else.

EDDIE

But, Katie, suppose he gets picked up.

CATHERINE

That's why we gonna do it right away. Soon as we finish the wedding he's goin' right over and start to be a citizen. I made up my mind, Eddie. I'm sorry. *To Beatrice:* Could I take two more pillow cases for the other guys?

BEATRICE

Sure, go ahead. Only don't let her forget where they came from.

Catherine goes into a bedroom.

EDDIE

She's got other boarders up there?

BEATRICE

Yeah, there's two guys that just came over.

EDDIE

What do you mean, came over?

BEATRICE

From Italy. Lipari the butcher—his nephew. They come from Bari, they just got here yesterday. I didn't even know till Marco and Rodolpho moved up there before. *Catherine enters, going toward exit with two pillow cases.* It'll be nice, they could all talk together.

EDDIE

Catherine! *She halts near the exit door. He takes in Beatrice too.* What're you, got no brains? You put them up there with two other submarines?

CATHERINE

Why?

EDDIE

(in a driving fright and anger)

Why! How do you know they're not trackin' these guys? They'll come up for them and find Marco and Rodolpho! Get them out of the house!

BEATRICE

But they been here so long already—

EDDIE

How do you know what enemies Lipari's got? Which they'd love to stab him in the back?

CATHERINE

Well what'll I do with them?

EDDIE

The neighborhood is full of rooms. Can't you stand to live a couple of blocks away from him? Get them out of the house!

CATHERINE

Well maybe tomorrow night I'll—

EDDIE

Not tomorrow, do it now. Catherine, you never mix yourself with somebody's else's family! These guys get picked up, Lipari's liable to blame you or me and we got his whole family on our head. They got a temper, that family.

Two men in overcoats appear outside, start into the house.

CATHERINE

How'm I gonna find a place tonight?

EDDIE

Will you stop arguin' with me and get them out! You think I'm always tryin' to fool you or sump'm? What's the matter with you, don't you believe I could think of your good? Did I ever ask sump'm for myself? You think I got no feelin's? I never told you nothin 'in my life that wasn't for your good. Nothin'! And look at the way you talk to me! Like I was an enemy! Like I—*A knock on the door. His head swerves. They all stand motionless. Another knock. Eddie, in a whisper, pointing upstage.* Go up the fire escape, get them out over the back fence.

Catherine stands motionless, uncomprehending.

FIRST OFFICER
(in the hall)
Immigration! Open up in there!

EDDIE
Go, go. Hurry up! *She stands a moment staring at him in a realized horror.* Well, what're you lookin' at!

FIRST OFFICER
Open up!

EDDIE
(calling toward door)
Who's that there?

FIRST OFFICER
Immigration, open up.
Eddie turns, looks at Beatrice. She sits. Then he looks at Catherine. With a sob of fury Catherine streaks into a bedroom.
Knock is repeated.

EDDIE
All right, take it easy, take it easy. *He goes and opens the door. The Officer steps inside.* What's all this?

FIRST OFFICER
Where are they?
Second Officer sweeps past and, glancing about, goes into the kitchen.

EDDIE
Where's who?

FIRST OFFICER
Come on, come on, where are they? *He hurries into the bedrooms.*

EDDIE
Who? We got nobody here. *He looks at Beatrice, who turns her head away. Pugnaciously, furious, he steps toward Beatrice.* What's the matter with *you?*
First Officer enters from the bedroom, calls to the kitchen.

FIRST OFFICER

Dominick?
Enter Second Officer from kitchen.

SECOND OFFICER

Maybe it's a different apartment.

FIRST OFFICER

There's only two more floors up there. I'll take the front, you go up the fire escape. I'll let you in. Watch your step up there.

SECOND OFFICER

Okay, right, Charley. *First Officer goes out apartment door and runs up the stairs.* This is Four-forty-one, isn't it?

EDDIE

That's right.
Second Officer goes out into the kitchen.
Eddie turns to Beatrice. She looks at him now and sees his terror.

BEATRICE

(weakened with fear)
Oh, Jesus, Eddie.

EDDIE

What's the matter with *you?*

BEATRICE

(pressing her palms against her face)
Oh, my God, my God.

EDDIE

What're you, accusin' me?

BEATRICE

(her final thrust is to turn toward him instead of running from him)
My God, what did you do?
Many steps on the outer stair draw his attention. We see the First Officer descending, with Marco, behind him Rodolpho, and Catherine and the two

strange immigrants, followed by Second Officer. Bea-
trice hurries to door.

CATHERINE
(backing down stairs, fighting with First Officer; as
they appear on the stairs)
What do yiz want from them? They work, that's all.
They're boarders upstairs, they work on the piers.

BEATRICE
(to First Officer)
Ah, Mister, what do you want from them, who do
they hurt?

CATHERINE
(pointing to Rodolpho)
They ain't no submarines, he was born in Philadelphia.

FIRST OFFICER
Step aside, lady.

CATHERINE
What do you mean? You can't just come in a house
and—

FIRST OFFICER
All right, take it easy. *To Rodolpho:* What street
were you born in Philadelphia?

CATHERINE
What do you mean, what street? Could you tell me
what street you were born?

FIRST OFFICER
Sure. Four blocks away, one-eleven Union Street.
Let's go fellas.

CATHERINE
(fending him off Rodolpho)
No, you can't! Now, get outa here!

FIRST OFFICER
Look, girlie, if they're all right they'll be out tomorrow. If they're illegal they go back where they came

from. If you want, get yourself a lawyer, although I'm tellin' you now you're wasting your money. Let's get them in the car, Dom. *To the men:* Andiamo, Andiamo, let's go.

The men start, but Marco hangs back.

BEATRICE
(from doorway)
Who're they hurtin', for God's sake, what do you want from them? They're starvin' over there, what do you want! Marco!

Marco suddenly breaks from the group and dashes into the room and faces Eddie; Beatrice and First Officer rush in as Marco spits into Eddie's face.

Catherine runs into hallway and throws herself into Rodolpho's arms. Eddie, with an enraged cry, lunges for Marco.

EDDIE
Oh, you mother's—!

First Officer quickly intercedes and pushes Eddie from Marco, who stands there accusingly.

FIRST OFFICER
(between them, pushing Eddie from Marco)
Cut it out!

EDDIE
(over the First Officer's shoulder, to Marco)
I'll kill you for that, you son of a bitch!

FIRST OFFICER
Hey! *Shakes him.* Stay in here now, don't come out, don't bother him. You hear me? Don't come out, fella.

For an instant there is silence. Then First Officer turns and takes Marco's arm and then gives a last, informative look at Eddie. As he and Marco are going out into the hall, Eddie erupts.

EDDIE
I don't forget that, Marco! You hear what I'm sayin'?

Out in the hall, First Officer and Marco go down the stairs. Now, in the street, Louis, Mike, and several neighbors including the butcher, Lipari—a stout, intense, middle-aged man—are gathering around the stoop.

Lipari, the butcher, walks over to the two strange men and kisses them. His wife, keening, goes and kisses their hands. Eddie is emerging from the house shouting after Marco. Beatrice is trying to restrain him.

EDDIE

That's the thanks I get? Which I took the blankets off my bed for yiz? You gonna apologize to me, Marco! Marco!

FIRST OFFICER
(in the doorway with Marco)
All right, lady, let them go. Get in the car, fellas, it's over there.

Rodolpho is almost carrying the sobbing Catherine off up the street, left.

CATHERINE

He was born in Philadelphia! What do you want from him?

FIRST OFFICER

Step aside, lady, come on now . . .

The Second Officer has moved off with the two strange men. Marco, taking advantage of the First Officer's being occupied with Catherine, suddenly frees himself and points back at Eddie.

MARCO

That one! I accuse that one!

Eddie brushes Beatrice aside and rushes out to the stoop.

FIRST OFFICER
(grabbing him and moving him quickly off up the left street)
Come on!

MARCO

(as he is taken off, pointing back at Eddie)

That one! He killed my children! That one stole the food from my children!

Marco is gone. The crowd has turned to Eddie.

EDDIE

(to Lipari and wife)

He's crazy! I give them the blankets off my bed. Six months I kept them like my own brothers!

Lipari, the butcher, turns and starts up left with his arm around his wife.

EDDIE

Lipari! *He follows Lipari up left.* For Christ's sake, I kept them, I give them the blankets off my bed!

Lipari and wife exit. Eddie turns and starts crossing down right to Louis and Mike.

EDDIE

Louis! *Louis!*

Louis barely turns, then walks off and exits down right with Mike. Only Beatrice is left on the stoop. Catherine now returns, blank-eyed, from offstage and the car. Eddie calls after Louis and Mike.

EDDIE

He's gonna take that back. He's gonna take that back or I'll kill him! You hear me? I'll kill him! I'll kill him! *He exits up street calling.*

There is a pause of darkness before the lights rise, on the reception room of a prison. Marco is seated; Alfieri, Catherine, and Rodolpho standing.

ALFIERI

I'm waiting, Marco, what do you say?

RODOLPHO

Marco never hurt anybody.

ALFIERI

I can bail you out until your hearing comes up. But I'm not going to do it, you understand me? Unless I have your promise. You're an honorable man, I will believe your promise. Now what do you say?

MARCO

In my country he would be dead now. He would not live this long.

ALFIERI

All right, Rodolpho—you come with me now.

RODOLPHO

No! Please, Mister. Marco—promise the man. Please, I want you to watch the wedding. How can I be married and you're in here? Please, you're not going to do anything; you know you're not.
Marco is silent.

CATHERINE
(kneeling left of Marco)

Marco, don't you understand? He can't bail you out if you're gonna do something bad. To hell with Eddie. Nobody is gonna talk to him again if he lives to a hundred. Everybody knows you spit in his face, that's enough, isn't it? Give me the satisfaction—I want you at the wedding. You got a wife and kids, Marco. You could be workin' till the hearing comes up, instead of layin' around here.

MARCO
(to Alfieri)

I have no chance?

ALFIERI
(crosses to behind Marco)

No, Marco. You're going back. The hearing is a formality, that's all.

MARCO

But him? There is a chance, eh?

ALFIERI

When she marries him he can start to become an American. They permit that, if the wife is born here.

MARCO
(looking at Rodolpho)
Well—we did something. *He lays a palm on Rodolpho's arm and Rodolpho covers it.*

RODOLPHO

Marco, tell the man.

MARCO
(pulling his hand away)
What will I tell him? He knows such a promise is dishonorable.

ALFIERI

To promise not to kill is not dishonorable.

MARCO
(looking at Alfieri)
No?

ALFIERI

No.

MARCO
(gesturing with his head—this is a new idea)
Then what is done with such a man?

ALFIERI

Nothing. If he obeys the law, he lives. That's all.

MARCO
(rises, turns to Alfieri)
The law? All the law is not in a book.

ALFIERI

Yes. In a book. There is no other law.

MARCO
(his anger rising)
He degraded my brother. My blood. He robbed my

children, he mocks my work. I work to come here, mister!

ALFIERI

I know, Marco—

MARCO

There is no law for that? Where is the law for that?

ALFIERI

There is none.

MARCO
(shaking his head, sitting)

I don't understand this country.

ALFIERI

Well? What is your answer? You have five or six weeks you could work. Or else you sit here. What do you say to me?

MARCO
(lowers his eyes. It almost seems he is ashamed)

All right.

ALFIERI

You won't touch him. This is your promise.
Slight pause.

MARCO

Maybe he wants to apologize to me.
Marco is staring away. Alfieri takes one of his hands.

ALFIERI

This is not God, Marco. You hear? Only God makes justice.

MARCO

All right.

ALFIERI
(nodding, not with assurance)

Good! Catherine, Rodolpho, Marco, let us go.
Catherine kisses Rodolpho and Marco, then kisses Alfieri's hand.

CATHERINE

I'll get Beatrice and meet you at the church. *She leaves quickly.*

Marco rises. Rodolpho suddenly embraces him. Marco pats him on the back and Rodolpho exits after Catherine. Marco faces Alfieri.

ALFIERI

Only God, Marco.

Marco turns and walks out. Alfieri with a certain processional tread leaves the stage. The lights dim out.

The lights rise in the apartment. Eddie is alone in the rocker, rocking back and forth in little surges. Pause. Now Beatrice emerges from a bedroom. She is in her best clothes, wearing a hat.

BEATRICE

(with fear, going to Eddie)
I'll be back in about an hour, Eddie. All right?

EDDIE

(quietly, almost inaudibly, as though drained)
What, have I been talkin' to myself?

BEATRICE

Eddie, for God's sake, it's her wedding.

EDDIE

Didn't you hear what I told you? You walk out that door to that wedding you ain't comin' back here, Beatrice.

BEATRICE

Why! What do you want?

EDDIE

I want my respect. Didn't you ever hear of that? From my wife?

Catherine enters from bedroom.

CATHERINE

It's after three; we're supposed to be there already, Beatrice. The priest won't wait.

BEATRICE

Eddie. It's her wedding. There'll be nobody there from her family. For my sister let me go. I'm goin' for my sister.

EDDIE
(as though hurt)

Look, I been arguin' with you all day already, Beatrice, and I said what I'm gonna say. He's gonna come here and apologize to me or nobody from this house is goin' into that church today. Now if that's more to you than I am, then go. But don't come back. You be on my side or on their side, that's all.

CATHERINE
(suddenly)

Who the hell do you think you are?

BEATRICE

Sssh!

CATHERINE

You got no more right to tell nobody nothin'! Nobody! The rest of your life, nobody!

BEATRICE

Shut up, Katie! *She turns Catherine around.*

CATHERINE

You're gonna come with me!

BEATRICE

I can't Katie, I can't . . .

CATHERINE

How can you listen to him? This rat!

BEATRICE
(shaking Catherine)

Don't you call him that!

CATHERINE
(clearing from Beatrice)

What're you scared of? He's a rat! He belongs in the sewer!

BEATRICE

Stop it!

CATHERINE
(weeping)

He bites people when they sleep! He comes when nobody's lookin' and poisons decent people. In the garbage he belongs!

Eddie seems about to pick up the table and fling it at her.

BEATRICE

No, Eddie! Eddie! *To Catherine:* Then we all belong in the garbage. You, and me too. Don't say that. Whatever happened we all done it, and don't you ever forget it, Catherine. *She goes to Catherine.* Now go, go to your wedding, Katie, I'll stay home. Go. God bless you, God bless your children.

Enter Rodolpho.

RODOLPHO

Eddie?

EDDIE

Who said you could come in here? Get outa here!

RODOLPHO

Marco is coming, Eddie. *Pause. Beatrice raises her hands in terror.* He's praying in the church. You understand? *Pause. Rodolpho advances into the room.* Catherine, I think it is better we go. Come with me.

CATHERINE

Eddie, go away, please.

BEATRICE
(quietly)

Eddie. Let's go someplace. Come. You and me. *He has not moved.* I don't want you to be here when he comes. I'll get your coat.

EDDIE

Where? Where am I goin'? This is my house.

BEATRICE

(crying out)

What's the use of it! He's crazy now, you know the way they get, what good is it. You got nothin' against Marco, you always liked Marco!

EDDIE

I got nothin' against Marco? Which he called me a rat in front of the whole neighborhood? Which he said I killed his children! Where you been?

RODOLPHO

(quite suddenly, stepping up to Eddie)

It is my fault, Eddie. Everything. I wish to apologize. It was wrong that I do not ask your permission. I kiss your hand. *He reaches for Eddie's hand, but Eddie snaps it away from him.*

BEATRICE

Eddie, he's apologizing!

RODOLPHO

I have made all our troubles. But you have insult me too. Maybe God understand why you did that to me. Maybe you did not mean to insult me at all—

BEATRICE

Listen to him! Eddie, listen what he's tellin' you!

RODOLPHO

I think, maybe when Marco comes, if we can tell him we are comrades now, and we have no more argument between us. Then maybe Marco will not—

EDDIE

Now, listen—

CATHERINE

Eddie, give him a chance!

BEATRICE

What do you want! Eddie, what do you want!

EDDIE

I want my name! He didn't take my name; he's only a punk. Marco's got my name—*to Rodolpho:* and you can run tell him, kid, that he's gonna give it back to me in front of this neighborhood, or we have it out. *Hoisting up his pants:* Come on, where is he? Take me to him.

BEATRICE

Eddie, listen—

EDDIE

I heard enough! Come on, let's go!

BEATRICE

Only blood is good? He kissed your hand!

EDDIE

What he does don't mean nothin' to nobody! *To Rodolpho:* Come on!

BEATRICE

(barring his way to the stairs)

What's gonna mean somethin'? Eddie, listen to me. Who could give you your name? Listen to me, I love you, I'm talkin' to you, I love you; if Marco'll kiss your hand outside, if he goes on his knees, what is he got to give you? That's not what you want.

EDDIE

Don't bother me!

BEATRICE

You want somethin' else, Eddie, and you can never have her!

CATHERINE
(in horror)
B.!

EDDIE
(shocked, horrified, his fists clenching)
Beatrice!

Marco appears outside, walking toward the door from a distant point.

BEATRICE
(crying out, weeping)
The truth is not as bad as blood, Eddie! I'm tellin' you the truth—tell her good-by forever!

EDDIE
(crying out in agony)
That's what you think of me—that I would have such a thought? *His fists clench his head as though it will burst.*

MARCO
(calling near the door outside)
Eddie Carbone!

Eddies swerves about; all stand transfixed for an instant. People appear outside.

EDDIE
(as though flinging his challenge)
Yeah, Marco! Eddie Carbone. Eddie Carbone. Eddie Carbone. *He goes up the stairs and emerges from the apartment. Rodolpho streaks up and out past him and runs to Marco.*

RODOLPHO
No, Marco, please! Eddie, please, he has children! You will kill a family!

BEATRICE
Go in the house! Eddie, go in the house!

EDDIE

(he gradually comes to address the people)

Maybe he comes to apologize to me. Heh, Marco? For what you said about me in front of the neighborhood? *He is incensing himself and little bits of laughter even escape him as his eyes are murderous and he cracks his knuckles in his hands with a strange sort of relaxation.* He knows that ain't right. To do like that? To a man? Which I put my roof over their head and my food in their mouth? Like in the Bible? Strangers I never seen in my whole life? To come out of the water and grab a girl for a passport? To go and take from your own family like from the stable—and never a word to me? And now accusations in the bargain! *Directly to Marco:* Wipin' the neighborhood with my name like a dirty rag! I want my name, Marco. *He is moving now, carefully, toward Marco.* Now gimme my name and we go together to the wedding.

BEATRICE *and* CATHERINE
(keening)

Eddie! Eddie, don't! Eddie!

EDDIE

No, Marco knows what's right from wrong. Tell the people, Marco, tell them what a liar you are! *He has his arms spread and Marco is spreading his.* Come on, liar, you know what you done! *He lunges for Marco as a great hushed shout goes up from the people.*

Marco strikes Eddie beside the neck.

MARCO

Animal! You go on your knees to me!

Eddie goes down with the blow and Marco starts to raise a foot to stomp him when Eddie springs a knife into his hand and Marco steps back. Louis rushes in toward Eddie.

LOUIS

Eddie, for Christ's sake!

Eddie raises the knife and Louis halts and steps back.

EDDIE

You lied about me, Marco. Now say it. Come on now, say it!

MARCO

Anima-a-a-l!

Eddie lunges with the knife. Marco grabs his arm, turning the blade inward and pressing it home as the women and Louis and Mike rush in and separate them, and Eddie, the knife still in his hand, falls to his knees before Marco. The two women support him for a moment, calling his name again and again.

CATHERINE

Eddie I never meant to do nothing bad to you.

EDDIE

Then why—Oh, B.!

BEATRICE

Yes, yes!

EDDIE

My B.!

He dies in her arms, and Beatrice covers him with her body. Alfieri, who is in the crowd, turns out to the audience. The lights have gone down, leaving him in a glow, while behind him the dull prayers of the people and the keening of the women continue.

ALFIERI

Most of the time now we settle for half and I like it better. But the truth is holy, and even as I know how wrong he was, and his death useless, I tremble, for I confess that something perversely pure calls to me from his memory—not purely good, but himself purely, for he allowed himself to be wholly known and for that I think I will love him more than all my sensible clients. And yet, it is better to settle for half, it must be! And so I mourn him—I admit it—with a certain . . . alarm.

CURTAIN

BANTAM WORLD DRAMA

Introducing a new library of living theater—from Euripides to Osborne. This series contains authoritative editions as well as fresh modern translations of the classics and important contemporary plays. Many of the plays contain introductions and commentaries by leading critics and scholars.

☐ **NT11** **TEN PLAYS BY EURIPIDES.** This volume includes all
   95¢ of the Greek dramatist's most important plays including MEDEA, TROJAN WOMEN, ELECTRA and ALCESTIS.

☐ **ST7** **THREE PLAYS.** The three most famous plays by
   75¢ Thornton Wilder, showing him at his audacious best —OUR TOWN, THE SKIN OF OUR TEETH and THE MATCHMAKER.

☐ **HT5** **CYRANO DE BERGERAC.** Here is Edmond Rostand's
   60¢ immortal play in which chivalry, wit, bravery and love are forever captured in the timeless spirit of romance. Translated by Brian Hooker.

☐ **NT2** **THE CRUCIBLE.** The world-acclaimed drama by
   95¢ Arthur Miller, author of DEATH OF A SALESMAN. This play focuses on the problem of the Salem witch trials and guilt by association.

☐ **NT3** **INCIDENT AT VICHY.** Arthur Miller's most recent
   95¢ play, a powerful and disturbing drama of ten men locked together by their common sense of doom.

☐ **NT4** **AFTER THE FALL.** Many critics have damned this
   95¢ play as a shockingly intimate portrayal of Arthur Miller's personal life with Marilyn Monroe. Others hail it as the most electrifying drama of our age.

☐ **NT1** **A VIEW FROM THE BRIDGE.** Arthur Miller's inter-
   95¢ nationally famous play about a man doomed to self-destruction by his own guilty desires.

☐ **HT6** **FOUR GREAT PLAYS BY IBSEN.** His world-renowned
   60¢ plays for all time—A DOLL'S HOUSE, THE WILD DUCK, AN ENEMY OF THE PEOPLE and GHOSTS.

☐ **NT8** **THE ENTERTAINER.** This shocking play by John
   95¢ Osborne, author of LOOK BACK IN ANGER and INADMISSIBLE EVIDENCE, is symbolic of a ruthless world desperately hell-bent on self-destruction.

AVAILABLE WHEREVER PAPERBACKS ARE SOLD

BANTAM CLASSICS

NOVELS

BRAVE NEW WORLD Aldous Huxley .... SC206 75¢

THE IDIOT Fyodor Dostoevsky .... WC297 85¢

CRIME AND PUNISHMENT Fyodor Dostoevsky .... HC140 60¢

MADAME BOVARY Gustave Flaubert .... FC178 50¢
(Translated by Lowell Bair—Introduction by Malcolm Cowley)

THE RED AND THE BLACK Marie Henri Beyle de Stendhal SC40 75¢
(Translated by Lowell Bair—Introduction by Clifton Fadiman)

CANDIDE Voltaire .... EC213 45¢
(Translated by Lowell Bair—An Appreciation by André Maurois)

PENGUIN ISLAND Anatole France .... NC247 95¢

ANNA KARENINA Leo Tolstoy .... NC180 95¢
(Translated by Joel Carmichael—Introduction by Malcolm Cowley)

THE ILIAD Homer .... HC208 60¢
(Translated by Alsten H. Chase and William G. Berry, Jr.)

EYELESS IN GAZA Aldous Huxley .... NC274 95¢

HENRY ESMOND William Makepeace Thackeray .... FC90 50¢
(Introduction by Lionel Stevenson)

THE AENEID Vergil (Edited by Moses Hadas) .... SC296 75¢

QUO VADIS Henryk Sienkiewicz .... SC181 75¢

WAR AND PEACE Leo Tolstoy .... NC291 95¢

THE GALLERY John Horne Burns .... NC279 95¢

DRAMA

TEN PLAYS BY EURIPIDES .... NT11 95¢
(Translated by Moses Hadas and John Harvey McLean—
Introduction by Moses Hadas)

THREE PLAYS Thornton Wilder .... ST7 75¢

THE CRUCIBLE Arthur Miller .... NT2 95¢

SEVEN PLAYS BY AUGUST STRINDBERG ... QC278 $1.25
(Introduction by John Gassner. Translated by Arvid Paulson)

FIVE PLAYS BY OSCAR WILDE .... NC251 95¢
(Introduction by Hesketh Pearson)

FIVE PLAYS BY GERHART HAUPTMANN ..... HC107 60¢
(Introduction by John Gassner. Translated by Theodore Lustig)

MACBETH William Shakespeare .... FC236 50¢
(Edited by Campbell, Vaughan & Rothschild)

JULIUS CAESAR William Shakespeare .... FC235 50¢
(Edited by Campbell, Vaughan & Rothschild)

(continued on next page)

ROMEO AND JULIET William Shakespeare............FC237 50¢
   (Edited by Campbell, Vaughan & Rothschild)

FOUR GREAT PLAYS BY IBSEN..................HT6 60¢

FOUR GREAT PLAYS BY CHEKHOV...........HC190 60¢

EIGHT EXPRESSIONIST PLAYS BY AUGUST
STRINDBERG (Translated by Arvid Paulson)..........QC261 $1.25

LOOK BACK IN ANGER John Osborne...............SC295 75¢

TEN EARLY PLAYS BY CHEKHOV..............NC283 95¢
   (Edited and translated by Alexander Szogyi)

GREEK DRAMA (Edited by Moses Hadas)..............NC285 95¢

COLLECTIONS

HENRY JAMES: FIFTEEN SHORT STORIES......SC84 75¢
   (Introduction by Morton D. Zabel)

75 SHORT MASTERPIECES: STORIES FROM THE WORLD'S
LITERATURE (Edited by Roger B. Goodman)............SC195 75¢

KEATS: POEMS AND SELECTED LETTERS......SC127 75¢

SWIFT: GULLIVER'S TRAVELS AND OTHER
WRITINGS (Edited by Miriam Starkman)...............NC290 95¢

THE FINEST STORIES OF SEAN O'FAOLAIN..QC267 $1.25

THE COMPLETE SHORT STORIES OF MARK
TWAIN (Edited by Charles Neider)......................NC259 95¢

COLERIDGE: POETRY AND PROSE...........RC281 $1.45
   (Edited by Carlos Baker)

THOREAU: WALDEN AND OTHER WRITINGS..NC292 95¢
   (Edited and Introduction by Joseph W. Krutch)

FIFTY GREAT POETS (Edited by Milton Crane).......QC288 $1.25

NON-FICTION

A HISTORY OF EGYPT J. H. Breasted...........QC232 $1.25

BEYOND THE PLEASURE PRINCIPLE Sigmund Freud SC197 75¢
   (Translated by James Strachey—Introduction and Notes by
   Dr. Gregory Zilboorg)

MY LIFE AND HARD TIMES James Thurber.......HC227 60¢
   (Introduction by John K. Hutchens)

YANKEE FROM OLYMPUS Catherine Drinker Bowen..NC205 95¢

THE INNOCENTS ABROAD Mark Twain.............NC215 95¢
   (Introduction by Alfred Kazin)

CITIZEN TOM PAINE Howard Fast ....SC268 75¢
